YOUR CHILD IS A PERSON

YOUR CHILD

A Psychological Approach

Professor of Psychiatry, New York Medical College

Associate Professor of Psychiatry, New York University School of Medicine

Research Professor of Pediatrics, Albert Einstein College of Medicine

NEW YORK

IS A PERSON,

to Parenthood without Guilt

STELLA CHESS, M.D.

ALEXANDER THOMAS, M.D.

HERBERT G. BIRCH, M.D., PH.D.

HE VIKING PRESS

First published in 1965 by The Viking Press, Inc.
625 Madison Avenue, New York, N.Y. 10022

Published simultaneously in Canada by
The Macmillan Company of Canada Limited

Library of Congress catalog card number: 65-24005
Printed in U.S.A. by Vail-Ballou Press, Inc., Binghamton, N.Y.

CONTENTS

Author's Note   *vii*

1: The Parents' Dilemma   3

2: The Search for Alternatives   16

3: The Long-Term Research Project   24

4: Child and Parent   35

5: To Bed if Not to Sleep   50

6: Breast or Bottle?   61

7: Feeding without Fuss   67

8: Graduating to the Cup   75

9: The End of Diapers   81

10: Establishing House Rules   87

11: A Code of Conduct   99

12: Sex and Modesty   *105*

13: New Situations   *112*

14: The Difficult Child   *122*

15: Playing in Character   *131*

16: A New Baby Arrives   *138*

17: Going to Nursery School   *146*

18: Learning in Style   *156*

19: The Working Mother: Not Guilty!   *166*

20: The "Late Bloomer"   *173*

21: The Handicapped Child   *179*

22: How to Spot Trouble   *187*

23: The Many Ways of Parenthood   *196*

Reference Notes   *205*

Index   *209*

AUTHORS' NOTE

We have written this book in order to communicate an approach to child development and child care that we believe can be useful to parents, teachers, pediatricians, and others concerned with nurturing the child's healthy psychological growth. The approach is based on the wide body of modern research that demonstrates the individuality of children.

In our view, personality develops as the result of a constant interaction between the child, with his unique way of reacting, and his total environment, in which the parents are highly influential elements. Neither the child's characteristics alone nor the parents' practices and attitudes alone provide an adequate basis for understanding psychological development, whether normal or deviant.

Much of our material is derived from our ten-year "longitudinal" research study in which we have followed the psychological development of 231 children from the earliest months of life onward. We have also drawn on our years of clinical work with parents and children, as well as on that of the large number of research and clinical workers who have contributed to our knowledge of child development.

The essential individuality of children is often overlooked in child-care books and in treatises on personality development. Many of these continue to be dominated by generalizations about what is "good" and what is "poor" child care that blur the facts about children and their individual functioning. Such generalizations may exert a pernicious effect upon the diagnosis of psychiatric disorders in childhood. Thus, in professional papers and reports, one comes across the statement, "To meet Johnny's mother is to understand his problem," a slogan that in practice all too often means, "Study the mother, not the child." To sum up a child in this fashion is to reach one's conclusions before gathering and examining the data. The resulting diagnostic plan fits the thesis, but does it fit the child?

Such generalizations also impair the ease and confidence with which parents can approach the responsibility of fostering the growth of their child's personality. Current knowledge of children and their development makes it possible to offer alternative approaches that can be helpful to both professional workers and children. Some of these alternatives we have already formulated in our book *Behavioral Individuality in Early Childhood* (New York University Press, 1963), as well as in a series of research papers published in various professional journals. The present volume represents a further effort in this direction for a broader audience.

Since problems of development change from infancy through the preschool years into the school years and in preadolescence, we felt that it would be overambitious to attempt to cover the whole age spectrum. Instead, we have chosen to deal most intensively with the period from infancy to first grade. Moreover, we have not tried to write a manual of child care, but rather to share with parents some principles of interrelationship important to psychological development that derive from current knowledge about children and parents. We hope that the present volume presents these principles clearly enough to enable parents to apply them for the benefit of their children and themselves.

The longitudinal study which provides the major part of the research findings reported in this book would not have been possible without the sustained cooperativeness and loyalty of the parents of our study children. We are happy to take this opportunity to express our gratitude to them. We appreciate also the cooperation of the many schools and teachers who made it possible for us to study the children in nursery and elementary school. Our debt to our research colleagues and assistants is also large.

Long-term behavioral studies of any scope are expensive. We

could not have carried out our own study systematically without financial support from a number of sources. Such aid was obtained initially from several private sources and from The Gralnick Foundation, and since 1960 the study has been supported by research grants from the National Institute of Mental Health, United States Public Health Service. The views expressed in this volume are, of course, entirely the authors' and should in no way be construed as reflecting the opinions of any of the agencies that have given the study financial support.

Special appreciation is due Jane Whitbread Levin, who worked tirelessly with us in preparing a manuscript which would present an extensive body of research findings and professional experiences in nontechnical form without sacrificing accuracy or content.

YOUR CHILD IS A PERSON

1 THE PARENTS' DILEMMA

Jimmy Smith was a planned baby. The day Mrs. Smith knew she was pregnant, she and her husband began reading enthusiastically about children. When Jimmy, a big fellow (eight and a half pounds), was born, his parents couldn't have been happier. They took him home when he was five days old, confident that with a minimum of pressure, a maximum of understanding, a schedule geared to his demands, and the reservoirs of affection they felt for each other and for him he would slide painlessly and a bit precociously from one stage of development to the next—a joy to himself and to all who knew him.

The child was three years old when his parents came to us. They were discouraged, unhappy, and full of self-blame. Neither of them had had more than two hours' sleep a night for weeks. The problem had been going on in more or less aggravated form from the moment Jimmy joined the family.

They had started feeding him on demand, as the books on baby care advised. But Jimmy didn't settle into his own routine after a few weeks, as the book promised. In fact, when he was six months old it was still impossible to predict from feeding to feeding when he would be hungry or how hungry he would be. When he cried at night, it was hard to tell whether he wanted food or attention. His parents would get up and warm a bottle for him, only to have him push the nipple out of his mouth and try to play. When they put him back to bed, he would start all over again.

They never dreamed of letting him "cry it out," for fear of

frightening him. Father and mother took turns trying to comfort the baby. The more they tried, the more he seemed to wake.

From what they had read, the Smiths concluded that Jimmy's sleeplessness came from anxiety and the anxiety came from them. In an effort to make the child feel secure, they practically cut themselves off from their friends. They had never left Jimmy with anyone but his grandmother, but by the time he was a year old they stopped going out at night altogether. It was no fun inviting people in. Jimmy insisted on climbing out of his crib and disturbing his parents at dinner.

One evening, in desperation, Mr. Smith decided to be firm. He put Jimmy to bed and told him to go to sleep. Jimmy came out of his room once and his father told him he'd spank him if he did it again. He cried and his father shut the door. He opened it and his father put him back to bed, spanked him, shut the door hard, and let him cry himself to sleep. This approach had a more deadly effect on domestic relations than going without sleep. Mrs. Smith accused her husband of acting like a Victorian dictator-father. She rescued Jimmy after three days, and the whole weary routine began again. Mr. Smith told us he had never stopped worrying about the dangerous effects of his one burst of firmness on his son. He said that he never again *showed* any anger. However, he realized that children *sense* resentment, and that this was probably behind Jimmy's obvious insecurity.

The Smiths and their pediatrician had worried over Jimmy together. The conscientious doctor was appreciative of his responsibility for the emotional as well as the physical health of his patients; advising parents about minor behavior problems was a routine part of his practice. He followed the new work in child development and psychiatry, just as he did pediatric medical news. His opinion confirmed the thinking of Jimmy's parents. Sleep disturbance in three-year-olds is a sign of anxiety, and the source of childhood anxiety is usually a disturbed relationship with the parents. The doctor told the Smiths that he thought the problems between them and their disagreement over how to handle Jimmy were increasing his own uncertainties about how much they loved him. He advised them to assure the three-year-old of their love for each other by being affectionate and avoiding any disagreement in

front of him. He told them to continue staying home at night until
the problem passed, and to respond lovingly and patiently whenever
the child cried at night.

Despite their best efforts, the prescription did not work. The
Smiths became more and more convinced that *they* had created a
deep-seated emotional problem in their son. Parents by enthusiastic choice, well read to the point of scholarliness in the field of
child development, these responsible, intelligent, affectionate
adults had done their best to practice what had been preached to
them, and they had failed.

Certainly many will recognize the combination of eager determination, gradual discouragement, eventual frustration and resentment, and overwhelming guilt and fear that the Smiths experienced
in their dogged efforts to make the current recipe for raising
healthy children work for them.

This syndrome is familiar not only to psychiatrists and pediatricians but also to psychologists, social workers, and educators. The
problem was highlighted in the 1960 report of a national mental-
health survey conducted by the Joint Commission on Mental
Health and Illness, in which thousands of Americans throughout
the country were interviewed extensively. Many parents expressed
worry and guilt about their inadequacy in relationships with their
children. The report said that "relationship problems and inade-
quacies" were particularly common among the better-educated and
younger parents. The authors remarked on the growing amount of
"psychological stress" that this kind of anxiety was causing in
parents.[1]

Why has the ever-increasing attention to the advice of child-care
experts failed to help parents care for children with relaxation and
confidence? Why, if anything, has the advice often seemed to create more fears than it allays? The reasons were vividly summarized
by a prominent child psychiatrist, Dr. Hilde Bruch of Columbia
University.[2] "Modern parent education," she said, "is characterized by the experts' pointing out in great detail all the mistakes
parents have made and can possibly make and substituting 'scientific knowledge' for the tradition of the 'good old days.' An unre-
lieved picture of model parental behavior, a contrived image of artificial perfection and happiness, is held up before parents who try

valiantly to reach the ever receding ideal of 'good parenthood,' like dogs after a mechanical rabbit.

"The new teaching," Dr. Bruch continued, "implies that parents are all-responsible and must assume the role of playing preventive Fate for their children."

She quoted a desperate young mother: "I cannot describe the torture of being censured and judged for everything you do for your child, every word you say to him, the very way you feel and even look at him."

Dr. Bruch also quoted Mrs. Millicent McIntosh, then President of Barnard College: "All the experts seem to be saying to young parents: 'Even the most innocent appearing act or a carelessly spoken word may "harm" a child or "damage" his future happiness. You hurt them by comparing them and praising them for being special. You hurt them by being too affectionate to them and by not being affectionate enough.' "

The mother is not only guilty before she is proved innocent; she is guilty before she even acts.

Behind this state of affairs is the vast and ever proliferating body of professional and popular material about children based on psychoanalytic theory. According to this theory, the parent exerts a decisive influence on personality from infancy onward. Freud, living in a patriarchal society, believed the father's role was paramount. More recent studies, deriving mainly from British and American sources, stress the ill effects of too much mother (overprotection) and of too little mother (rejection and deprivation). These concepts are characteristic of the current focus on the strategic role of the female parent. Because the mother literally wields the power of life and death, what she feels, what she does, and how she does it are vitally important from the start and continue to be all through early development.

Development, according to Freud, centers around the evolution of the instinctual drive for pleasure (*libido*) with which babies are born. Presumably, libido manifests itself in various forms throughout childhood, reaching its ultimate expression in adult sexuality. The first form of expression is the oral phase, manifested in infancy, which is followed by the anal stage, and then by the so-called genital, or oedipal, stage. According to the theory, the development of personality depends upon the manner in which the child moves through the various stages. This, in turn, depends upon the manner in which the parents treat the child at each stage.

In the oral phase, so we are told, the infant's pleasure comes from sucking. Too little or too much sucking, too early or too late weaning, frustrations by delays or irregularity in feeding—all can produce problems. In the anal phase, the child's satisfaction is derived from bowel action. When his spontaneous performance is interfered with too early in life, when he is made to feel that what gives him pleasure is distasteful to others, when he is forced to give up these delights before he is ready, the belief is that his total personality development may be seriously affected. In the oedipal, or phallic, phase, the child's genitals give him pleasure. The parent of the opposite sex is the love object. If all goes well, the child abandons this primitive love idyl in the course of his fifth or sixth year and (if a boy) identifies with his father, abandons all conscious thought of incest, and is on his way to mature heterosexual development.

A parent who accepts this theory will inevitably be confronted with difficulties. How does the mother promote healthy progress from phase to phase? How does she help the child adjust to the demands of the society he has to live in without causing so much frustration that his growth is hampered? How does she know when encouraging *social* development (drinking from a cup, going to the toilet, etc.) will interfere with *total* development?

The authorities are often less than helpful. They caution parents not to frustrate the child's instinctual needs, but at the same time warn that too little restraint leaves him helpless in his battle to direct and control his instincts.

How does a mother know when reasonable restraint becomes frustration, or when frustration is good or bad? How can she decide when permissiveness results not in freedom but in license? The experts urge common sense as a guide in judging what is too much sucking or not enough, too little toilet training or too much for a given child. They also suggest using the baby's behavior as an objective measure of the suitability of the parent's practice. If the child is happy, and if he is progressing smoothly toward more self-mastery, more mature expression, more sociable behavior, his mother is presumably doing all right. If he isn't, she can infer that she has mishandled him, that her efforts have adversely affected his development.

With such vague guidelines, the mother often feels as if she were walking on eggs, alert for the sound of a crack. Should the baby cry when a stranger smiles, or run for Daddy's bed when his father is not looking, or stop drinking his usual quota of milk after weaning, the mother begins to search for causes in herself. If she can't find the source of trouble in the way she has diapered, aired, played with, cuddled, and disciplined the baby, she worries about her attitudes, her femininity, and her marriage.

If she can't find anything wrong consciously, she begins to speculate about her unconscious. She accepts the view that the unconscious is a repository for the wishes, thoughts, feelings, and impulses that were forbidden in childhood. Even though repressed, they may dominate conscious behavior in subtle ways beyond the individual's control.

The mother's unconscious is described as particularly active in her relations with her children. Having a child presumably activates the unconscious material repressed in one's own childhood. A mother might be unconsciously reminded of her childhood jealousy of a younger brother, mistreat her son, and favor her daughter. If her father had wanted her to be a boy, she may unconsciously indulge her own son as a projection of the male she wanted to be. Did her father or mother give her ideas about women's inferiority that lead her to reject her baby daughter? Or does she just fear helplessness, which the baby symbolizes?

It has been argued that these feelings, whether expressed or not, or known to the mother or not, can be "caught" by young children like measles and leave psychic scars. For example, one authority hypothesizes a process of "contagion" through which the mother's feelings are transmitted to the infant. This is said to explain how "a mother's feeling state, including altogether unconscious material, exerts a marked effect upon the baby's response." [3] Juvenile delinquency, too, is blamed on the parent's unconscious. "The parent or parents, usually unconsciously, sanctioned and fostered the child's acting-out of the parents' poorly integrated forbidden impulses." [4]

The concept of the unconscious has been repeatedly invoked to account for difficulties in establishing routines. This is neatly illustrated in relation to toilet training. The mother has difficulty in establishing the balance between training and spontaneity that some experts say will contribute positively to the child's development. Her life is now further complicated when she is told that "the direct contact with the anal activity of the child—the seduction thus coming from the child—stimulates the mother's own conflicts and induces her at times to relinquish her role as mother. Temporarily she can thus gratify her old pleasure in uncontrolled soiling through identification with the child." [5]

Presumably, the stable, secure, and well-adjusted mother—or the well-analyzed one—might hope that the unconscious feelings *she* lets through to the child are desirable ones. But since they are after all unconscious, how can she be sure?

Even if she feels competent to deal with her own unconscious, there is still the vast, uncharted area beneath the surface of her child's outward actions to cope with. She must be sure that she is picking up the right cues from the child's behavior and then correctly analyzing what they reveal about the state of his real and unconscious feelings. Thus, if Annie, aged five, says she doesn't want to visit Susie, is it because she doesn't like her or can't stand Susie's mother? Is it because she is afraid to leave her own mother? Or even more sinister, is it because her ego is so weak that she is fearful of making the first reaching steps towards friendship?

If answers to such questions suggest emotional weakness in the child, the mother must turn again to a study of faults within her own unconscious. For example, if she decides Annie is afraid to make friends, she must consider the possibility that her own timidity has infected the child or, more deviously, that her anxiety has unconsciously made her drive Annie to be social before she was old enough to be so independent.

Mother is really groping blindly in a wilderness of dangers. The more she searches for daylight, the more obscurity she finds. Even if she understands the child's needs, her unconscious reactions may prevent her from meeting them. Thus, child raising is a "task not easily achieved by the average mother in our culture," concludes Dr. Margaret Mahler, a highly regarded authority on the psycho-analytic approach to child development. Mothers who are trying to bring up children normally, in spite of "their own unconscious conflicts about their maternal role," she adds, are indeed in a "pre-dicament." [6]

Just about every mother is in such a "predicament" if one can judge from a recent study of twenty-two mothers randomly se-lected in the Boston area. The psychoanalytically oriented investi-gators found that only one of the twenty-two women studied could qualify as a "mature mother." [7]

In an effort to allay some of the fears and doubts that this de-manding formula for bringing up children has created in parents, educators constantly issue reminders that good old-fashioned love makes up for many conscious and unconscious defects. Dr. James L. Hymes, Jr., a prominent authority on early childhood educa-tion, says, "Ultimately the answer has to come from inside each one of us. We have to feel comfortable about what a youngster is doing in order to make him feel comfortable." [8] This is helpful as long as the child prospers, but if he develops a problem, even a minor one like shyness with strangers or a rebellious phase, the mother is back where she started. If only she loved the child enough, if only she felt comfortable enough to make *him* feel com-fortable, the problem never would have arisen.

No complaint could be made if these theories were scientifically sound and had in fact added to the depth and detail of our under-standing of behavior and development. One could then merely say that applying the lessons has been hard for mothers and that in the name of progress sacrifices and adjustments are to be expected. If the advantages were real, the hardship entailed could be over-looked. But does this approach to bringing up children really work? Is it really sound? For an answer let us return to three-year-old Jimmy Smith.

In two sessions with his parents, we were able to obtain a pic-ture of Jimmy that was markedly different from what his parents felt, thought, and worried about, and what they imagined was go-ing on. We found that Jimmy's irregular sleeping habits had been present in his first weeks, before his parents even had a chance to be responsible for them. His appetite and his bowel function had also been erratic from the beginning.

We investigated more closely, but found no signs of the deep fears that the parents and pediatrician thought were keeping him up at night. He had gone to nursery school without a backward glance at mother. He had been accustomed to stay with both grandparents overnight very early in life and never protested. He had asked to go home with the friends he had made in the park long before most of the other children wanted to leave their mothers. When he came to our office, he left his mother in the waiting room, answered questions easily, and, after examining all the toys we had to offer, soon settled down with blocks and played with them all during our talk.

We couldn't believe his sleeplessness had anything to do with insecurity. We guessed it might be the simple product of his modest need for sleep, his irregular pattern of sleeping, and his parents' failure to regulate him for *their* convenience and sanity.

We talked to Jimmy's mother about *Jimmy,* rather than about theories. We discussed what he did and what he had done from the start, instead of delving into Mrs. Smith's feelings, ideas, and interpretation of Jimmy. We suggested that he might be a boy with a very irregular biological clock and very little need for sleep, and not the victim of his mother's rejection and his father's resentment. When they were told this, the parents' relief was dramatic. It was as if we had lifted a jail sentence.

After reviewing the way they had handled Jimmy, we planned a new course. They had been telling him he had to go to sleep. He couldn't sleep on command. We suggested concentrating on getting him to stay in bed. They couldn't change his pattern of sleeping any more than they could make him hungry at regular intervals, but they could see that his habits didn't interfere with the comfort and convenience of the rest of the family.

When they put him to bed they were to say, "You don't need to go to sleep, but you must stay in bed. You can look at books, play with your toys, or draw, but don't get out of bed."

The parents followed this prescription and made progress. Then Jimmy came down with a cold. The pediatrician paid him a visit, heard about the new regime, and reacted with horror. Again he warned the parents about the dangers of leaving Jimmy alone with his presumed fears at night. "I strongly advise you to stay with him until he falls asleep," he recommended.

The mother's fears revived. Next night she went in to the boy's bedside to carry out the pediatrician's order. Jimmy was playing with toy soldiers on the bedcovers. He looked up and asked her what she was going to do. "I'm going to help you go to sleep," she said.

Jimmy looked puzzled. "You never did *that* before," he said. "I don't want you."

Jimmy's unequivocal tone convinced his mother that she could safely continue with the regime that we had worked out. In a month Jimmy's problems at bedtime were over, and he was none the worse for having had some limits imposed.

As the Smiths' pediatrician quickly pointed out, this didn't for a minute prove that his interpretation of Jimmy's behavior was wrong. Nor can we hope that Jimmy's subsequent happy development will convince other pediatricians, psychiatrists, psychologists, educators, and social workers that their view of child development is mistaken. One case history does not invalidate a theory. Nevertheless, we have seen enough Jimmy Smiths to wonder about the evidence on which the psychoanalytic approach is based.

Psychoanalytic theory has relied heavily on parents' reports of their children's development. To do this is natural in a discipline which is clinically based. However, a number of systematic checks on the accuracy of mothers' memories reveal that mothers *mis*-remember what happened to their children.[9] In addition, their memories seem to "edit" the child-care methods they used, to make them conform more closely to "right" methods. For example, since late weaning and toilet training and permissive attitudes in discipline are the mode, mothers "remember" weaning and toilet training the child later than they actually did.

This tendency is documented in a recent review of studies of parents' recall, "The Reliability of Developmental Histories."[10] The report finds that mothers are particularly unreliable about questions on which psychoanalytic theory puts most stress. They distorted memories of the child's feeding and toilet training, his steps toward independence, and his symptoms of aggression.

Parents often come to us with their own diagnosis of a child's problems. They can supply the early experience which, according to their interpretation of psychoanalytic theory, might account for the present difficulty. But when an accurate check of the child's past history is possible, it often develops that the crucial incident has never taken place.[11]

One may well ask, what of the thousands of adults who, during psychoanalysis, remember mistreatment and mishandling by their mothers as the cause of their neuroses? An answer has been indicated by Dr. Jerome D. Frank, a professor of psychiatry at Johns Hopkins University, in his book *Persuasion and Healing*. Dr. Frank shows how much such memories, insights, free associations, and even dreams are influenced not by the facts of history, but by the ideas and theories of the analyst, even though both patient and doctor may not realize that this is happening.[12]

Clinical experience, too, fails to support the theory that the quality of the mother's care is the sole or even in all cases the most important determining influence in the child's development. It is of course more usual for healthy parents to have healthy children and for the emotionally ill to produce sick children, but this relation is by no means inevitable. We see loving mothers whose children have problems. And we see very sick mothers with healthy and well-adjusted children who are apparently immune to the mother's pathology and the erratic patterns of care.

Experienced child psychiatrists confirm these findings. "There is not a direct quantitative relationship between pathology in a parent and pathology in a child. . . . This presents a great problem for the development of any pertinent generalizations concerning the influence of parents on children," observes Dr. Helen Beiser of the Institute for Juvenile Research in Chicago, a leading center for studies in child psychiatry.[13]

Research does not support the claimed relation between the specific ways a mother handles her child and his subsequent development. In 1949, Harold Orlansky of the Department of Anthropology at Yale University analyzed investigations of the effects on child development of the mother's child-care practices. The findings were largely negative.[14] Several reviews in the 1950's came to the same conclusion. Of special significance was a report in 1956 of a study of parent-child relations by Dr. Edith Jackson, Clinical Professor of Pediatrics and Psychiatry at the Yale University Medical School, and her associates. The authors reported: "Not only was no significant relationship found in the first year between maternal practice and child behavior in the areas of feeding and socialization, but when the mother's first-year practices were related to the child's behavior in the second year to determine whether a delayed effect could be shown, no significant relationships appeared." [15] Several more recent studies have substantiated these findings. A typical conclusion is that "we can at present hardly even guess which kind of family produces which kind of person." [16]

These studies and reviews are offered not to minimize the mother's importance to her children but to call attention to the fact that there is no proof at all that the mother's conscious and unconscious influence is unilaterally decisive.

Of course, children are not immune to their mothers. Frequently their problems seem to reflect poor care. On the other hand, what looks like "bad" mothering often shows up, after careful investigation, to be the mother's confused reaction to a difficult child, rather than a primary cause of the child's problems. Any conscientious young mother who has been persuaded that she is uniquely responsible for her children's healthy development is bound to feel guilty and anxious when a child is difficult. When the problems persist, her feelings sometimes explode in anger at the child. The mother then looks like the villain. Actually, the picture is a much more complex one. The problem is not the parent's, but the parent's *and* the child's, and results from a pattern of interaction between the two.

The role in which most contemporary theorists of child development cast the mother makes it hard for her and hard for her children. What's more, the evidence indicates that she has been *mis*cast. No matter how seriously she takes the demand on her for omnipotence, and no matter how omnipotent the performance she turns out, there is no guarantee that the act will come off. All too often the child fails to reflect the best parents' most studious try for perfection.

Both the published evidence and our own experiences have convinced us that prevailing psychoanalytically based theories of child care are wrong. But an unsound theory does not wither away by itself. Its influence will continue until alternative viewpoints appear that are based on more substantial scientific evidence.

Are there such alternative theories of child development?

2 THE SEARCH FOR ALTERNATIVES

"Joe is so slow." "Louise never forgets." "Betty is so sensitive." "Ben just can't keep his eye on the ball." "If only Hal could get started." "George is a worker." "Tom always gives up."

These casual characterizations illustrate the way we acknowledge human differences. From time immemorial philosophers and scientists have wrestled with the problem of explaining such individuality. What makes one person develop differently from another? What are the reasons for the easy, smooth psychological growth of one child and the stormy, disturbed development of another?

Over the ages, two types of answers have been offered. One explains individual differences on the basis of inborn characteristics already present at birth and most usually assumed to be inherited. This *constitutionalist* view, as it is called, goes back to antiquity. For example, the ancient Greek physician Hippocrates classified people into four types of personality based on differences in their "body humors." To this day the terms that he used—sanguine, choleric, bilious, and phlegmatic—are used colloquially to describe different personality types.

The *environmentalist* view, on the other hand, traces individual differences to the influence of environment and experience. This approach also goes back to antiquity, but was perhaps first formulated systematically by the seventeenth-century English philosopher John Locke. He asserted that the child at birth was a *tabula rasa,* a clean slate, on which experience then wrote its story.

In the nineteenth century the constitutionalist view prevailed. Even such complex characteristics as honesty, bravery, laziness, wickedness, introspection, and exhibitionism were attributed to heredity: "He has the same kind of honesty as his father." "He's sowing his wild oats just like his Uncle Harry did." "He's a born liar." Mental illnesses were inherited through a "bad seed." Many types of abnormal behavior were attributed to "constitutional weakness."

This was a fatalistic view of behavior. Not the child, but his predetermined character, was seen as father to the man. Parents and society at large could try to curb the growing child's inherently bad traits and encourage his good ones by moral training and discipline. But, in general, environment was thought to have little influence, good or bad, on the way a person developed.

Such a static view of human nature clashed with the growing belief in progress and change fostered by the dramatic advances of science and technology during the nineteenth century. It was contrary to Darwin's thesis that evolution is basic to all forms of life. It was finally discredited by the weight of scientific evidence that many traits once considered hereditary are largely the result of experience.

The work of three men in the early part of the twentieth century —the Austrian psychiatrist Sigmund Freud, the Russian physiologist Ivan Pavlov, and the American psychologist John B. Watson —focused the scientific spotlight on the importance of environment in child development.

Freud, for all his theories of biological drives and instincts, was primarily an environmentalist. He believed, from his clinical study of psychiatric patients, that the adult personality reflected the motives and emotions of the parents and the kind of care given in early life. Difficulties in weaning could produce an "oral personality," wrong toilet training might result in an "anal personality," problems in the oedipal stage could result in many forms of neuroticism, including hysteria, phobias, and homosexuality.

Pavlov's approach was radically different. His work was primarily experimental and physiological, and demonstrated that animals and men develop new reflexes in the brain as the result of their experiences. He felt that these "conditioned reflexes," as he called them, were the basis for complex habits and behavior patterns developed during the individual's growth as a person.

As we have seen in Chapter 1, Freud's followers in the psychoanalytic movement have continued to concentrate on the part played by the parents in determining the child's development. The parents, and especially the mother, are often seen as all-responsible. Their unconscious attitudes influence the child as if by contagion. Too much frustration of the child and too little frustration are both bad.

One special group of psychoanalysts, called the neo-Freudian cultural school, have emphasized the importance of social and cultural influences in shaping the child's development. Competitive traits are seen to arise not only from competition within the family but also from the competitive nature of society. Personality traits of stinginess and hoarding are said to come not only from the "anal personality," but from the social emphasis on the importance of money and the "market place." The best-known exponent of the culturalist view is the psychoanalyst and philosopher Erich Fromm, but this concept of child development is held by many others as well.

In the first decades of the twentieth century, John B. Watson at Johns Hopkins University emphasized the role of learning mechanisms in development. As founder of the school of behaviorism, he believed that planned habit training could mold the child in any desired direction. "Give me a dozen healthy infants, well-formed, and my own specified world to bring them up in, and I'll guarantee to take any one at random and train him to become any type of specialist I might select—doctor, lawyer, artist, merchant-chief, and yes, even beggarman and thief, regardless of his talents, penchants, tendencies, abilities, vocations, and race of his ancestors." [1]

This view was both one-sided and oversimplified. It failed to take into account the influence of differences in children's individual capacities and their reactions to environment. It also overlooked the fact that even if a parent followed behaviorist teaching to the letter and applied constant and consistent reinforcement to produce desired learning, he could never isolate his children from the reinforcement of the larger environment and the counterlessons it might teach. Moreover, as our knowledge of the learning process has grown, it has become increasingly difficult to apply any simple concept of learning to the development of the child.

A separate line of investigation was developed by Dr. Arnold Gesell, a pediatrician at Yale University, who described stages of behavior and development in children. He based his behavior calendar on observation of groups of children at various age levels beginning with infancy. Focusing upon general features of development common to all children, he found that the young behave in characteristic fashions at each stage. Further, behavior changed from one age to another and seemed to follow a well-defined sequence.

From his studies, Gesell concluded that physiological and behavioral growth proceeds at a certain pace and that behavior at any age is an expression of the child's state of maturity and adaptation to the environment. Babies crawl when coordination makes crawling possible. They stand when they can pull themselves up, throw furniture around when large muscles are developed, and so on. Social behavior also appeared to follow a clear developmental sequence. Gesell identified cheerful stages, withdrawn stages, outgoing stages, friendly stages, negative and uncooperative stages, all of which, he believed, express the capacity of children to meet the social demands of the environment at a particular age.

Gesell's detailed descriptions of normal behavior at closely spaced age levels were a comfort to parents. He made most behavior seem normal, and added the reassuring promise that no matter how bad a given stage might seem to be, it would go the way of those before it. A similar emphasis on general developmental features is seen in the work of the Swiss psychologist Jean Piaget on the growth of reason in children. When can they grasp cause and effect? When can they make abstract judgments? When and how do they achieve mastery of mathematical processes? Piaget found that these intellectual functions seem to develop by orderly stages and sequences as children grow older, just as Gesell had found with behavior.

Thus, our concepts of the forces operating in the child's development have been enlarged from many directions. Freud called attention to the emotional and motivational factors involved in early parent-child relationships. The culturalists emphasized the important influence of society at large. Pavlov demonstrated the conditioned reflex and its place in patterning behavior. Watson and the later learning theorists explored the role that training and learning play in determining behavior patterns. Gesell's work called attention to the schedule of neurological and behavioral maturation, and the part it plays in the process of development. Piaget showed that intellect has its own sequential course of growth.

None of this work, however, fully explains the richness and variety of human personality. We learn how children in general act from one age to the next. We learn how their thought processes develop. We discover something about the neurological mechanisms involved when children take the manifold steps toward maturity. But we still have to account for the striking individual differences in children. Why do equally normal children learn differently? Why does one child master certain tasks and lessons easily, while another child experiences great difficulty? Why is one child from a given environment placid and resilient, and another child from the same environment intense and easily upset?

Modern biology has suggested a solution. Physical growth and development of any living species is now increasingly recognized to be a product of the interaction between constitutional factors *and* environment. Development is not divided between the two, so much coming from nature and so much from nurture. The two sets of forces constantly influence each other. Whether it is an individual's height, his weight, his brain, his bone structure, or his blood vessels, the final result is always the product of the interaction of nature and nurture. The influence of one cannot be accurately evaluated without a simultaneous understanding of the other.

This concept of interaction is as important for the understanding of behavior as it is for the understanding of physical structure and physiological function. To assess the effect of any experience on a child—weaning, toilet training, the birth of a younger sibling, going to school, or watching movies or television—requires knowledge not only of the event, but simultaneously of the child's characteristic reactions.

Events in themselves can have no developmental meaning. Only if the child has characteristics which lead him to respond to an event in a given way can its influence on development be understood. Consequently, the environment is first filtered by the child's own characteristics. Children with different characteristics, therefore, will be affected differently by the same objective occurrence.

Not only does the child screen his environment, he also influences it. Thus, it is not alone the parents who influence the child, but the child who influences the parents. The child, by his own nature, "conditions" his environment, at the same time that the social and cultural environment affects him. In short, there is a continual effect produced by the child on his world, as well as by his world upon him.

Applying this approach to a study of child development might yield the answers we are seeking: Why do similar parents have children who turn out quite differently? Why do different parents sometimes have children who end up alike? Why has no single set of rules for bringing up children worked for all?

Suspecting that the answer—in personality development as in biological growth—lay in the interacting influence of the child's individuality, the parents' characteristics, and the broader social environment, we decided, about fifteen years ago, to begin a study of child development that would allow us to analyze, as exactly as possible, the interaction of nature *with* nurture.

We believed that to do this kind of study we would need to gather comprehensive information about each child's individual traits of behavior and analyze how the environment affected his development. Proving that babies are different sounds like laboring the obvious. Any nurse who has ever presided over a hospital nursery knows that babies act differently from the moment that they are born. Any reasonably perceptive mother, too, can pick up distinct variations in the way each of her successive offspring goes about the business of living. Nevertheless, while various students of child behavior have called attention to the concept of individual differences, the implications of this basic truth for development have not been systematically pursued.

Freud speculated that children might be born with different quantities of libido and suspected that these variations might influence their reactions to frustrations. Pavlov called attention to individuality in the development of conditioned reflexes and theorized that these differences reflected different kinds of nervous systems, the patterning of which might account for individuality in man and other animals. Gesell, despite his emphasis on general patterns, observed individual differences in children which he felt played a significant part in personality formation.[2] In the 1930's similar observations were made in pioneer studies by Dr. Mary Shirley at the University of Minnesota.[3]

However, when we decided to embark on a systematic investigation of individual differences, the state of knowledge in this field was fragmentary and sparse. The Mid-Century White House Conference on Children and Youth reported in 1950: "All who have had the opportunity of watching children of like ages have been impressed with the high degree of individuality which each one shows. Even as newborn infants they differ not only in such physical characteristics as weight and height, but also in the manner in which they react to events. . . . At present, however, factually tested knowledge concerning individual differences among children is so scarce that there is doubt of the wisdom of including it in this report." [4]

Perhaps stimulated by this call for action, a number of reports began to appear in the 1950's. They identified individual differences in physiological and behavioral function, particularly in very young infants. Variations in general activity level, threshold of sensory response, perceptual reactions, sleeping rhythms, feeding behavior, social responsiveness, autonomic reactivity, biochemical levels, and electroencephalographic (brain-wave) patterns were described.[5]

In the last few years, the psychological and psychiatric literature has reflected the increasing general interest in these questions. Especially noteworthy has been the study by Dr. Lois Murphy and her associates at the Menninger Foundation. In *The Widening World of Childhood,* Dr. Murphy reports that children have unique ways of coping with the stresses and challenges of their environment, and she considers ways in which individual coping methods can influence adjustment and development.[6]

Other investigators have catalogued differences of attainment in I.Q. level, athletic prowess, and artistic talent. Still other studies have explored differences in motivation and goals, the "why" of behavior.

In our own study we have made a systematic attempt at a comprehensive and continuing analysis of individuality in behavior from infancy through the early school years. We set out to study *how* each child behaves in all conceivable kinds of situations and activities. This *how* of behavior has been characterized in many ways: it is referred to sometimes as "behavior style," sometimes as "response pattern"; the simplest and clearest collective term that may be applied to it is "temperament."

To analyze temperament and its interaction with other factors, we obtained information that would enable us to describe infant behavior in a comprehensive and systematic way. We sought to establish a basis for judging whether initial temperament was persistent or varied as the child grew up. We also tried to characterize the interactive processes between temperament and environment as they affected development.

We spent five years testing various research methods and reviewing impressions gained from years of professional and personal observations of growing children. In 1956, satisfied with the procedures we had developed for getting our data, we launched the New York Longitudinal Study of Child Development.

3 THE LONG-TERM
RESEARCH PROJECT

The outlines of our study were dictated by the need to find answers to the questions that we have been raising. How do babies differ in their style of behavior, their temperament? To get a clear picture we had to observe different babies doing the same kinds of things early in life. We had to get from their mothers a detailed description of the ways in which the babies acted and reacted as they went through the typical routines of the first months. These reports and our observations helped to show us their initial individuality.

How does individual temperament develop? What role does it play in personality development? What part does the environment play in the shaping of personality? Is the mother's approach to the baby fixed, or does the baby's temperament affect the mother's handling? Answers to these questions required careful and continued study of the children as they grew. As we followed their behavior in the ordinary situations that all children meet daily, the differences in individual reaction patterns began to be sharply defined.

We also wanted to pinpoint the dynamics of the child's developing personality. To do this, we sought detailed information on the specific circumstances in which the child's behavior occurred. We obtained reports that told us what the parents were doing when a given behavior appeared, what preceded the baby's reaction, what the parent did to influence this reaction, how the baby responded to being influenced.

For example, if a mother said that her six-month-old child woke up crying several nights a week, we asked:

"Did anything specific wake him, such as a noise, or light in the room?"

"When he woke up what did you do?"

"What did he do then?"

"Did he stop crying?"

"Did he start to cry again when you put him down?"

This kind of material told us not only what both mother and child did, but how they did it, when they did it, and how they affected each other's behavior: the nature of the interaction between them.

There are now 231 children in the study. These children, whom we have been following since they were young babies, now range from three to nine years in age. The first 136 come from eighty families in the New York area. Their parents for the most part are native-born, college-educated business and professional people. The parents' ideas about child care are fairly similar and their styles of life much the same. Against this homogeneity of background, the children's behavioral differences tend to stand out in striking fashion.

Since 1960, we have also studied 95 children of Puerto Rican working-class parents, to see whether our original conclusions about temperamental individuality would be consistent for children raised in a different social and cultural environment.

We have also been able to follow two or more brothers or sisters in a number of the families, as well as nine sets of twins. This has given us an opportunity to watch the development of children raised in the same general way and see how their differences, plus differences in their parents' reactions to them, affect their development.

We have done our best to insure unbiased results. During the first three years we relied on interviews with the parents, for the obvious reason that no one else is in a position to supply as detailed and comprehensive a picture of the child as they can. We took many precautions to insure both objectivity and accuracy. The interviews took place often enough so that the parents' reports covered events in the child's life that were still close enough in time and memory to be clearly remembered.

Descriptive reports of what children did, rather than interpretive accounts of their behavior, also improved the accuracy and objectivity of the information. For example, if a mother said that her child did not like his first solid food, we asked her to describe his actual behavior. We were satisfied only when she gave a description such as, "When I put the food into his mouth he cried loudly, twisted his head away, and let it drool out."

If we asked what a six-month-old baby did when his father came home in the evening, and his mother said, "He was happy to see him," we pressed for a detailed description: "As soon as he saw his father he smiled and reached out his arms."

Interpretations of behavior were discounted for several reasons. First of all, different observers can agree on what they see a child *do* much more readily than they can agree on the interpretation of the meaning, feelings, or motivation of the action. Furthermore, different babies may "like" the same food or activity but express this feeling quite differently. For example, one may smile slightly, another may coo, and a third may shriek with laughter. An interpretation misses the richness and variety of behavior.

Our interviewers are always receptive, and they are trained never to express a critical attitude toward the parent. This is essential in getting forthright reports from parents.

To see how well these precautions for getting faithful reports worked, we sent independent observers into each of fifty-five families in the study to record the child's behavior. We then compared their direct observations with the parents' reports and found a high level of agreement between the two.

When a child reached nursery-school age, another independent observer, who did not know the child's history, visited his class at least once each year and stayed long enough to get a detailed picture of how he behaved when working and playing alone and with other children, resting, eating, listening to music or stories, going to the park, or playing games. His teachers, too, from nursery school on, gave us annual reports on the details of his typical behavior in school. When the child was three years old, and again when he was six, we gave him standardized psychological tests. His behavior before, during, and after these tests was also observed and recorded in detail.

Having obtained this wealth of behavioral description, we avoided imposing any interpretations on the material based either on our own or on any other preconceived theory of child development. Our objective, instead, was to sift out the similarities and differences among children and then try to assess the influence of such factors as the child's initial temperament, his mother's reaction, special environmental circumstances, and special methods of child care. We found that at each age level children showed clear patterns of individuality.

The patterns may be illustrated by comparing several infants. Todd was an easy child to introduce to a widening range of foods; he accepted almost everything and ate huge quantities. Susan, on the other hand, spat out or pushed away every new food; but after her mother persisted in offering it to her for a few days, she generally came to accept each one in turn. Cheryl also refused all new foods at first. When her mother persevered in giving them over and over, the baby gradually came to eat some, but continued to refuse others.

Interestingly, each infant approached not only new foods but other new situations in a characteristic way. Todd loved his bath from the beginning, while Susan's first response to the bath was to kick and scream. Susan did not *begin* to lie quietly in the water for two weeks, but by the third week she began to kick gently, gurgle and splash, and even to cry when removed from the tub.

Peggy's mother could set her clock by the child's sleepiness, knowing that it was either one o'clock and time for the afternoon nap, or eight o'clock and time for Peggy's evening bedtime. Joey, on the other hand, was completely unpredictable. One day he might take two naps. The next, his eyes might not close all day long, even though he lay obediently in his crib, cooing and talking to himself through rest period. One night he might fall asleep at six, another night at ten. He might cry two or three times during the night or sleep through. He had no regular pattern.

In our study we were able to classify these individual characteristics of the children's behavior under nine headings. Let us consider each of these criteria in detail.

1. *Activity level*

Some babies were from early infancy onward much more active than others. Even in the period toward the end of feeding, when most babies were quiet and sleepy, they moved their arms, lifted their heads, kicked, or—if they were on their backs—moved their whole bodies till the covers were off. This went on right to the moment their eyes shut. Even when asleep they frequently moved from spot to spot in the crib. Their mothers could never turn away for a moment if these infants were on the bathinet, for fear they would squirm off. Diapering them was a problem because they twisted and turned so much.

In contrast, the quiet babies tended to lie where they were placed and moved both little and slowly. Sometimes they were almost as still when awake as when asleep. Often only their eyes moved.

2. *Regularity*

We found that babies differed in the regularity of their biological functioning. Some seemed to have been born with built-in alarm clocks. By the second or third week they were hungry at regular times. Their mothers could plan the day's activities around the babies' predictable nap and feeding times. Their bowel movements were also regular.

Other babies were quite different. There was no telling when they would be hungry, how hungry they would be, or when they would be hungry next. Their naps might be short one day and long the next.

3. *Approach or withdrawal as a characteristic response to a new situation*

Young babies have new experiences every day. There is the first bath, the first taste of orange juice, the first solid food. New people are constantly coming into their lives. They go out in the carriage for the first time. A bonnet is put on. They get a first injection. They go into a playpen for the first time.

The category of approach-withdrawal characterizes the child's *initial* reaction to any new stimulus pattern, be it food, people, places, toys, or procedures. Some babies had no trouble with these new experiences. For example, in the first bath they took to the water like ducks. Others, however, did not splash and kick, or coo and play with their mothers; they screamed when put into the bath for the first time. They spat out many new foods at first, cried at a stranger, and reacted negatively to strange places.

4. *Adaptability to change in routine*

Babies' routines are constantly shifting. When they begin solid foods, the number of meals gradually declines. In the first days they are almost constantly sleeping or dozing, but then their naps become less frequent.

In considering a child's adaptability we are concerned with the step-by-step development of responses to new situations or altered routines. In contrast to approach-withdrawal, we are not concerned with the initial response, but with the ease or difficulty with which this response can be modified in socially desirable ways.

Some babies shifted easily and quickly with a changing schedule. They could readily learn to eat a little earlier or later and go to bed at a different hour. In general, they changed their behavior to fit in with the pattern the mother wanted to set. With others a change in routine brought fussing and crying or screaming and kicking. Only with difficulty and much repetition were mothers successful in shaping the child's behavior. On occasion these babies did not adapt at all. Instead, it was the mother who frequently adjusted to the child's pattern rather than continue the unsuccessful struggle to impose her preferences.

5. *Level of sensory threshold*

Some mothers felt that they were fortunate because they could have a houseful of visitors without worrying at all about awakening the baby. Babies with a high "sensory threshold," as it is called, did not startle at loud noises; bright lights didn't bother them. Whether clothes were smooth or rough, wool or cotton, hot or cold, made little difference. They were not particularly discriminating about food. Their mothers could easily disguise something the baby didn't like by adding it to something "good." They did not react to being wet or soiled.

At the other extreme were babies who cried the moment they soiled. There were sensitive ones who, even in the first weeks, woke up when a light was turned on in the room or a door latch clicked. Some literally shuddered at even a whiff of a disliked food. A slight sound would attract their attention, and their eyes would move toward it. One mother could always tell when her husband was home, because her six-month-old could hear his footsteps in the hall outside the apartment and would start to coo and kick.

Response to pain varied. One baby could bang his head hard against the crib bars without a whimper. For another a slight bump would bring howls of discomfort.

6. *Positive or negative mood*

Mothers' reports contained descriptions of the children's moods. Here are some excerpts from one report: "Susie cried when she woke up. She cried after she was put down. She cried when the door banged. She whimpered until she fell asleep." Clearly, these all describe negative mood. Another report might be interspersed with bits like these, characteristic of positive mood: "She smiles before she gets her bottle. She gurgles when she's being undressed for her bath. She splashes and coos in the water. She babbles and hums when she wakes up." We called positive everything from gentle cooing to loud gurgles, from smiles to giggles. We labeled negative everything from gentle fussing or crying to sobbing in great gasps.

When a child gave no sign that he was either for or against what was happening, we scored his reaction as neutral. For example, a mother took her baby out of his playpen, put on his snowsuit, and put him in his carriage. He just let it happen, neither gurgling nor smiling, not frowning or crying. We judged each baby's mood by whether positive or negative reactions were preponderant.

7. *Intensity of response*

One baby let his mother know he was hungry with a loud, piercing cry. Another baby cried softly. These two examples show the range of intensity of the children's reactions. Both children are crying, but one is doing so with a considerably greater expenditure of energy than the other. When a behavior is characterized by a high level of energy expenditure, it is judged as intense. When the energy expenditure is low, the response is considered mild. One baby may open his mouth for a second spoonful of food he likes without any other movements. This is a response of mild intensity. On another occasion he might open his mouth, turn toward the dish, and strain actively toward the spoon with his whole body. Such a response is one of high intensity. The child of preponderantly low intensity smiles gently, but his more vigorous companion chortles, gurgles, and kicks when he is happy.

The intensity of response does not relate to whether the child is showing positive or negative mood. It refers to the energy expressed in his behavior.

8. *Distractibility*

Some babies seemed able to concentrate better than others. The way they took their bottles is a good illustration. The nondistractible child would usually drink until he was full, no matter what was going on around him. The ringing of the telephone bell would cause only the most momentary pause in sucking. He would ignore passers-by or even active efforts to win his attention. The distractible infant, crying when hungry or hurt, could be diverted with a rattle or by being picked up or talked to. The nondistractible one continued to bellow until he tasted milk. No amount of juggling, cooing, or stroking would alter his direction of behavior.

9. *Persistence and attention span*

It may sound strange to talk about persistence in a newborn baby, but this quality can be seen even in very young infants. We observed great variation in the ability of different babies to continue an activity in the face of difficulties or to resume it after interruption. Some children sucked very persistently at the nipple with small holes, even if little milk was coming through. Others gave up quickly. The persistent infant kept trying to reach a toy that was out of reach. The nonpersistent one tried for only a few minutes. If he objected to having his face washed, the persistent baby kept pulling his face away. The nonpersistent baby gave in after a brief struggle.

The child with a long span of attention gazed at his cradle gym intently for half an hour. The same baby, a year later, would stick with one toy for quite a long period. A baby with a short attention span, on the other hand, would focus only briefly on any activity or aspect of the environment. At a year and a half he might flit from toy to toy, spending very little time with any one of them.

The child's preponderant pattern of functioning in these nine categories may be called his *temperament*. There is nothing mysterious about temperament. It merely represents a statement of the basic style which characterizes a person's behavior. Some students of behavior have divided psychological functioning into three parts which they call the *what,* the *why,* and the *how*. The *what* refers to the content of behavior, including intelligence, skills, aptitudes, and talents. The *why* relates to motivation, or the reasons for behaving in a given way. The *how* refers to temperament—the manner in which the *what* and the *why* are expressed.

During infancy, information about temperament has to be obtained primarily from the child's behavior in the routines of daily functions: sleeping, feeding, dressing, eliminating, bathing, moving about. When children grow to be toddlers and then go to nursery school, their lives become more complex. Our ways of gathering information about them must expand with their horizons. Therefore, as the children grew older, we extended our inquiries to include the gathering of information on *how* the children behaved when they met strangers, played with new toys, were sick, were left alone, went to the hospital, moved from one house to another, drank from a cup, went to a playground, rode a tricycle, got a pet, stayed with sitters, were toilet trained, learned to read, or went to stores, restaurants, hotels, or a circus.

To make our knowledge as valid and as representative as possible, we picked situations in the child's life that were typical for his age. For example, to find out how active a child was (very quiet, moderately quiet, active, restless, hyperactive), we might ask a mother how her two-month-old baby moved in the bath, or how he moved when diapered. We would ask the mother of a three-month-old baby to tell us how much he pumped his legs, what attempts he made to turn over. When the child was two years old, we asked how many times he fell off his chair during a meal, how he played in the park, or how he acted during his first haircut. When the child was five, we found out how he used a tricycle. Did he run or walk when he saw something he wanted? What were his favorite games? How vigorously did he play at them? How much did he climb on furniture? How many times did he get lost when taken to a large store because of running around?

If we wanted to discover how intensely a child reacted at two months and to identify his mood, we got a description of his bath. Did he scream, howl, stiffen, turn red? Did he sob? Did he whimper? Did he startle but make no noise? Did he smile or laugh? Did he take it in stride, deadpan? Later, we asked questions about the degree of enthusiasm or distaste for new foods. When he was two, we found out how he expressed pleasure or displeasure when given a new toy (ranging from quiet acceptance to effusive hugs, kisses, and thanks, or—on the negative side—from noncommittal rejection to loud expressions of displeasure).

We investigated his play behavior at five. Did he play without much fighting or laughter or talk? Did he complain loudly when displeased? Did he shout with glee? When older, did he cry when he struck out at baseball? Did he look disappointed but say nothing? Did he remain apparently unruffled? Did he shout, "You're a cheater," or quietly turn away?

We found that all the 136 middle-class children and the 95

working-class Puerto Rican children could be scored on all the nine categories of temperament in the first few months of life. Records supplied by parents later—at the six-month, two-year, and six-year period—could be scored in the same way. Descriptions of behavior obtained from the nursery-school teacher and from direct observation of the child in school or during standard psychological tests also yielded useful data on each child's individual organization of temperament.

Infants do differ in temperament, even in the first few months of life. We described their differences systematically in terms of the nine qualities of reactivity explained earlier.

All children change as they grow older, but most of them continue in important ways during the later years to exhibit some of the qualities of behavior they showed in early life. In many children, the similarities between infant behavior and behavior when they started school was striking. Others showed changes in behavioral style which appeared to be the reflection of parental handling or special experiences. In short, we found temperament very important in development, but not fixed or immutable.

How does the temperament we can detect in the child's first week express itself as he develops? Why do two babies who start out to be very much alike develop quite differently? What are the influences, particularly the parent-child influences? Biographical records of some of our children are a copious source of information on this subject.

4 CHILD AND PARENT

There is a two-way circuit between parent and child. Each is constantly sending messages and receiving replies. The messages influence the replies, and the replies in their turn touch off new messages. Does the parent get the child's messages? How appropriate are the replies? The influence of this complex interaction on the course of the child's development is illustrated in the following sketches of initially similar children whose development has been divergent.

The "Slow Warmer-Up"

Ralph and Jerry were very much alike as babies. In any new situation their initial reaction was to back off quietly. With each new experience—the first bath, the first food, a new person handling them—they either turned solemn or quietly refused to participate.

Both children would turn away from a new food or let it dribble out of the mouth. When older, both might run behind mother's back if a strange person greeted them. But after tasting the new food over and over again, or seeing the new person many times, both children would gradually come to accept the innovation. In short, both boys took a long time to warm up, but given an opportunity to re-experience new situations without pressure, each gradually came to show mild and quiet, positive interest.

By the time they were five years old, however, the two children behaved very differently. Ralph was a well-adjusted member of his kindergarten group. He looked forward to going to school, greeted his playmates pleasantly, and visited back and forth with his friends after school. He continued to be placid rather than exuberant, even with good friends, but he was clearly contented and happy. When he visited in a new home, went to a new place, or met new children, he still took a long time to function easily. But both he and his family had learned that his shyness would wear off in time, and everyone was willing to wait.

Ralph's parents had come to understand very early that his hesitancy about accepting the unfamiliar needed to be honored. They found that rushing him didn't work. For example, an enthusiastic uncle applied pressure to get him to play at the edge of the surf on his first trip to the beach. The usually placid Ralph cried and kicked. Once out of his uncle's arms, he ran away and refused to go near the water again that day. On the basis of past experience with Ralph, his parents made no further efforts to get him into the water. At his own speed, however, he got a little closer to the water's edge each day, until at last he put his toe in. Finally, moving at his own pace, he became one of the more active sand-castle-brigade members at the water's edge.

Jerry's early functioning was much like Ralph's. His parents, too, didn't rush him. They didn't care how long it took him to begin to eat solid food or change from four to three feedings a day. But his mother's attitude changed when she started to take Jerry to the neighborhood playground and he reacted to the new situation and strange faces by holding back and clinging. The mother was dismayed, since to her, as to many other American mothers today, this moment was a big test of social maturity and healthy personality development. She felt that Jerry had failed this test and was sure that the other mothers in the playground were blaming her for having such an "anxiously" timid baby. They probably were.

These concerns made her lose sight of the fact that Jerry's initial reaction to the playground was typical of his behavior in all new situations. Instead of holding the child in her lap or giving him a familiar toy to play with near her until he warmed up to the new setting, she began to push him insistently to play "like the other little boys." The more she pressured, the more he clung. The more he clung, the more pressure she applied. Finally, she gave up taking him to the playground at all.

When Jerry entered kindergarten, he cried and clung again. In class he rarely spoke above a whisper. When the other children moved from one activity to another, Jerry stayed on the outskirts watching. Before school each morning he clung to his mother, asking over and over again who would bring him home. He had in fact, become the anxious, fearful child his mother dreaded.

Although Ralph and Jerry continued to be alike in basic temperament, their social functioning was radically different. Ralph's parents had recognized how he operated, and accepted it. With their understanding and patience, he became a relaxed, cheerful member of his play and school groups. Jerry's mother, although she had recognized the initial resistance of her child to unfamiliar situations, had disregarded his needs when she felt social pressure. In her self-concern she actively pressed him to do what for him was temperamentally unsuitable. As a result, he became an unhappy, whiny child, frightened of new experiences and contented only when moving in a limited and very familiar little world.

The Difficult Child

Jane and Tommy kept their respective mothers constantly on the go. Their likes and dislikes were never in doubt. They either howled long and loudly, or they beamed and chuckled and laughed. Their first reaction to a new situation, however, was generally a negative one. They screamed every time there was a change of routine. It took them both an enormously long time to accept any changes.

They were hard babies to care for in other ways as well. Nothing seemed to go the same way from day to day. One could not predict their naptimes, nor how much they would want to eat or when. In fact, it wasn't even possible to prophesy what their reactions to people and places might be from day to day. They were intense, preponderantly negative in mood, irregular, and slow to adapt.

The two children grew up quite differently. Jane's mother seemed inexhaustibly patient and consistent with her. When Jane was one, two, and even three years old, a denial in the supermarket would turn her into a screaming, kicking little fury. But her mother almost never blew up. She would patiently pick Jane off the floor, take the purchases to the check-out counter, and go home without screaming or fussing back at Jane. These tactics were markedly successful, and neighbors were frequently amazed to see the youngster playing contentedly a few minutes later. With proper handling Jane could forget that there had ever been a commotion just as quickly as she could register her howling discontent.

Little by little, as she grew, she became more of a social human being. When, time after time, her violent demands brought firm, consistent, and quiet removal from the social scene, her tantrums diminished. In time they began to look more and more like token attempts at self-assertion. Fortunately, neighbors and relatives took their cues from Jane's parents. They let her scream, but refused to let her inconvenience others. They were pleasant and ungrudging when the child made her lightning switch to positive behavior.

In nursery school Jane was most obstreperous at the beginning of the term. The teacher, who had been alerted by Jane's mother, behaved with firmness and calm. As a result, after a brief period of settling in, Jane became a generally cheerful and cooperative little girl. In kindergarten she continued to show occasional intense reactions or stubborn refusals to participate. Although these sometimes took the teacher by surprise, she generally remembered the history of the child's behavior and responded appropriately.

Jane still has stubborn sulks at home from time to time. If she is sent to her room, she slams things around for a few minutes. Then silence falls. When her parents investigate, they usually find her engrossed in play.

Tommy behaved much like Jane in the beginning. However, his parents reacted to him very differently. They felt harassed from the beginning. When the child's pattern persisted as he passed his first, then his second, and finally his third birthday, they grew increasingly upset. Nothing seemed to satisfy Tommy, even though they were constantly trying to make him happy. They gave in to his demands, reasonable or unreasonable. If he wanted a toy in the supermarket, his mother bought it quickly to avoid trouble. But no matter how much his parents tried to satisfy him, every excursion, every visit, indeed every play period was marked by some commotion. His mother's indulgent attitude had limits. She could take just so much and then would explode, screaming: "You always make trouble. Nobody can satisfy you." She would also make endless threats, but would not carry them out. Tommy's father kept aloof from this frantic interplay between mother and child. One fuss from his son and Daddy left him to his own devices. As time went on there was less and less contact between the two. Both parents were convinced that Tommy was impossible to please or satisfy. Indeed, this had become true, not only at home, but at play and in school.

The Easy Child

Both Greg and Pammy were "good" babies. They slept well, accepted almost every new food without fuss, adjusted to changes in schedules quickly and contentedly. Both children were moderately active and, as they grew older, seemed equally happy swinging on the Junglegym or sitting quietly listening to a story. They were models of good behavior even on long automobile trips.

Both children usually welcomed new faces. When they were playing outdoors it was not unusual for strange passers-by to stop for a brief chat with these youngsters who smiled and said, "Hi," to everyone. Neither child had any trouble in opening a conversation: "See my new shoes," or "I have a baby brother," or "I'll play with you" were enough to invite a friendly interchange. By the time Greg was three, he played regularly with the neighborhood children, visiting them in their houses and being visited in turn.

To settle the inevitable tussles over toys, his mother and father made clear-cut rules. The child accepted them readily and followed them much as he had accepted and adapted to earlier routines and experiences. He learned quickly that there was a time to share and a time to insist that the toy was his by right. Although he had many ideas for games, he was willing to play his friends' games, too, as his parents had taught him.

The range of Greg's play was almost limitless. He would enjoy wild, active, follow-the-leader games, and quiet sit-down play. There were also long sessions when he built with his Tinker Toys or crayoned or painted. Though he had not attended nursery school, he acted like a veteran by the end of the first day in kindergarten. In first grade he made rapid progress in school subjects, eagerly following the teacher's instructions.

Pammy also got along very smoothly with a group of friends when she was three. Usually charming and pleasant, she knew how to take turns on the slide and never threw sand in the sandbox.

Her parents handled her quite differently from the way Greg's had handled him. Pammy's father and mother recalled their own childhoods as unpleasant. They had been constantly chided because whatever they did was not considered good enough—it had to be superlative. They were therefore determined to spare their own child this kind of unhappiness.

When Pammy was a baby, they played with her endlessly and were completely captivated by her cheerful responsiveness. When she was a year old, they found themselves incapable of making the usual first demands: "Don't touch" or "Help put the blocks away." Whenever they tried tentatively to do so, Pammy's charm would always divert them from their purpose. When the child was asked to help clean up after play, she would side-step the request by saying, "Play peekaboo" or "Hold me a little." The parents would abandon their purpose and start playing with Pammy.

When Pammy, aged two, was asked to brush her teeth, she would engage her parents in a discussion on toothbrushes. "My toothbrush is pink. Have you ever had a pink toothbrush? Can I have a toothbrush like Daddy's?" And the parents would smile, answer the questions, and ignore the fact that their original instruction had been, "Come brush your teeth."

If Pammy showed her mother a picture she had made, mother's response was always, "Isn't it fun?" If she asked her father to see her perform a new feat in the park, his invariable reaction was, "Wonderful."

Pammy got the impression that everything she did was charming and pleasant. At three, she was a favorite with older children. She liked to be the cuddly, cooed-over object she was at home. Actually, her social style had not progressed much beyond infancy.

The social immaturity had more general adaptive consequences. Thus, on the standardized I.Q. test given her at this time she measured borderline defective. The examining psychologist was sure that the score did not truly reflect her potential ability. It didn't. Pammy didn't score well because she was so busy turning the test into a game that she never performed what she was asked to do. When she was told to string beads in the manner explained by the tester, Pammy *talked* about beads. "I have beads like these at home. Which beads do you like best? I like the blue and red together."

By the time the psychologist had persuaded her to *string* the beads, the child had forgotten the directions, if she had ever bothered to hear them.

When she went to kindergarten she had even more trouble recognizing and following instructions. By second grade she had learned so little about the rules of play that the other children were no longer interested in her. She didn't follow the rules of the games they played and could be counted on to help her partner or her team to lose. Her formal learning was equally inept.

At seven, although she was still an amiable child, she was beginning to be a lonely one. She was also beginning to feel more and more stupid, even though her intellectual capacity was normal. Her temperamental capacity for easy adaptability had resulted in her adapting all too well to the style of functioning her parents had encouraged. She was pleasant and wanted to please, but she no longer knew how. Her father's and mother's undiscriminating acceptance of her every move had prevented her from finding out how to work and play when others made the rules or to progress in mastery and responsibility. Her babyish ways are anything but charming now.

The Highly Active Child

Two children in our study shared a talent for moving more actively and quickly than most children. When Larry and David were little babies, their arms and legs seemed to be in constant motion. When they got to be toddlers, no corner of the house was safe from them. Their sudden darts in unanticipated directions when they were on the street kept their parents constantly on the alert. In view of their ability to climb to dizzying heights in two seconds, it was amazing how few accidents they had.

At the playground they always made a beeline for the Jungle-gym. In a moment they would be hanging from the top rung. It was futile to put things on high shelves. Nothing was ever really out of their reach. Sharp objects seemed to hold a special fascination for them. No matter how carefully the kitchen knives were put away, these toddlers always seemed to find them. But for some unaccountable reason, minor burns, scratches, and an occasional scraped elbow or knee were the only pain their misadventures ever cost them.

When the children were three years old, the arrival of a friend to play was a signal for shrieking activity. This meant wild running around and jumping from furniture. Later, standing on heads, cartwheels, and more daring acrobatics predominated during play sessions.

Larry's parents labeled him "the monster" very early in life. But this was really a term of endearment. They seemed to enjoy him even when they were holding their breath for his safety. They reported his extraordinary physical exploits good-humoredly and even with pride as he grew.

On a nursery-school expedition Larry's teacher noticed that the youngster was missing just as the group was about to cross a street. The four-year-old boy had shinnied up a lamppost while the others were waiting for the light to change.

When Larry was eight, his gym teacher had a similar experience with him. The teacher was showing the class how to climb a rope and then get down. Just as he was about to demonstrate how to get a foothold and take a few steps, he noticed that his class was missing one member. Larry was again on high, this time at the top of the rope.

"What are you doing? You weren't supposed to go up there," the teacher said.

"Now he tells me," Larry replied as he slid to the floor.

Although Larry wasn't always the easiest child to be responsible for, he was pleasant and responsive. By the time he was two, his parents had accepted the fact that he would get into forbidden places, look with his hands, and think with his feet. Despite a number of frightening incidents, the youngster's father and mother were not alienated by his behavior. As Larry grew in understanding they were able to impress a few rules upon him, and he did his best to follow them. Of course, his best was not always very good. In active games he tended to be rough. Other children sometimes got hurt, but despite this, he was well liked and the doorbell and the phone rang frequently for Larry.

David's parents may have had less stamina, less humor, or more bric-a-brac. They would have been appalled at parents who called their child "the monster." No terms of opprobrium were ever applied to David. However, the parents were constantly annoyed at the streak of lightning they were harboring in their house. Admonitions like "Sit still," "Don't touch," "Put that down," and "Stop running" were constantly directed at the child from the time he could climb. Half of these commands were impossible for him to follow despite his good intentions. He just had to move.

In the welter of correction it became impossible for David to distinguish between important and unimportant admonitions, and between acceptable and forbidden activity. As a result, he began increasingly to ignore all attempts to curb his activity. By the time he was three, he developed into a negative child who got attention from his parents primarily by provocative teasing.

When he went to school at five, he was always blamed for any rough play that developed, not only by his mother and father, but also by the parents of his playmates. The more he was criticized, the bigger grew the chip on his shoulder. He began to play rough, pushed ahead in line, disregarded other people's comfort. By the age of eight, he made little or no effort to control his behavior, anywhere, at any time.

More and more desperate for ways to discipline him, his parents withheld privileges. He was deprived of television for week after week, put in his room on countless occasions, and not allowed to have friends in to play. Gradually he developed an I-don't-care attitude. His parents complained: "We can't find anything that matters to him to take away." As soon as he developed an interest his parents used it as a club. By the time he was ten he gave up *having* interests of which they could deprive him.

The Persistent, Nondistractible Child

Susie's parents were lively, ebullient people who always seemed filled with enthusiasm. Susie's temperament was so different from theirs that they found it difficult to understand this solemn, determined daughter. There was no real problem when she was a baby. She fussed actively, but usually only when she was uncomfortable, and her parents rarely had trouble finding out what was wrong and fixing it.

As Susie grew older, however, her parents found the child increasingly hard to fathom. They were never sure that they knew when she was pleased, but when she was unhappy it was plain enough. At such times she whined and fussed monotonously. This grated on their nerves. The youngster was never what they would call "really enthusiastic." She would work steadily and quietly at a chosen activity for long periods. For example, at the age of three, she would build with blocks or work on jigsaw puzzles for hours at a stretch. She even tried to do things that were beyond her, like asking to be shown how to sew a button on a piece of cloth. At first she failed, but she continued to struggle over this task until at last she succeeded. Her persistence went unnoticed by her parents, who wanted her to "lighten up."

When she was four, her mother took her to a puppet show. She sat gravely watching the show with no change of expression until the curtain fell. Then she whined through the intermission, asking over and over, "Why is the curtain down? Why don't they begin?" and paid no attention to her mother's explanation. Her fussing stopped at once when the curtain went up again, but resumed when the play ended. She whined all the way home. Her mother was convinced that the outing had been a failure, until she heard Susie telling the entire play, scene by scene, to a friend the next day.

Mother and father both felt that happy interludes were few and far between. They couldn't take Susie's undemonstrative nature. They couldn't appreciate her quiet absorption. And her fussiness became more and more irritating to them. Her mother would flare up: "Aren't you ever satisfied? I'm not going to take you out any more because you don't really like anything I do for you." Susie wilted and retired at these attacks.

Her father's patience was even shorter. He exploded at the first sign of whining. It seemed to him that to get angry was the only way to change her pattern of conduct.

Susie had two little brothers who were expressive, alert, and quick-moving. They were exactly the kind of children the parents enjoyed and understood. As they began to get a greater and greater share of favorable attention, Susie made less effort to win approval and affection.

Quiet persistence was her strength, but it earned her little positive recognition from her father and mother. By the time she was in kindergarten she prefaced almost every activity she tried with, "I'm stupid. I don't do anything right." When she had a chance to choose an activity she became absorbed quickly and kept at it until she had finished it successfully. However, her periods of interested involvement became rarer and rarer. Her parents' insistence that she didn't know how to do anything but whine destroyed her spirit and confidence. She whined less, but she became a truly sad and depressed child.

Ellen's development was different because her parents reacted differently. In part, they shared her capacity for burying herself in what she was doing. When the child was three, her mother once said: "If Ellen gets interested in something it's as if she were swimming under water. She's so lost to what's going on around her." As a matter of fact, when Ellen was six she entered an underwater distance contest in a children's swimming meet. One by one the other children's heads popped up along the length of the pool. No Ellen. She came up at last at the far end. Her mother asked her how she had stayed under so long. She said solemnly, "You were supposed to go as far as you could. I couldn't go any further than the end."

Sometimes, of course, her persistence was inconvenient. One day when she was four she decided to learn how to tie her shoe-laces just when the family was leaving the house to visit Grandma. Ellen was picked up despite her protest and put into the family car. This failed to distract her. She paid no attention to her grandmother or to the other guests during the family visit, but kept on trying to tie her shoes until she at last succeeded.

The family appreciated her tenacity. When she was a year old, her mother could settle her in the playpen with magazines to tear up and toys to play with, assured of two or three hours of free time ahead.

She was a delightful companion for her father. When he took her to the zoo, she became so absorbed in the animals that it was usually a problem to get her to leave. She was capable of staging tantrums to prove that she wanted to stay. But this was only a minor inconvenience to parents who understood what it was like to be uprooted from work that was intensely absorbing to them, and each episode was quickly over and forgotten without residual rancor.

Her persistence and powers of concentration were great assets when she was old enough for school. She could concentrate and apply herself seriously. Her self-esteem, fostered by her parents' respect, made her an effective worker. The particular interaction of her temperament with her environment insured Ellen's successful development.

The fact that children are different is not a reason for parents to abdicate and let the young raise themselves as their individuality dictates. But it does mean that the child's temperament should be taken into account when trying to plan ways to guide his growth. It may also suggest to child-development specialists that, when problems appear, neither the child, as he is, and as he has been from infancy, nor his parents' attitudes and practices alone, are sufficient to explain his behavior. Both the child and his parents in their interaction must be examined before a diagnosis is made and treatment recommended.

In our study, one little boy named Scotty began having temper tantrums when he got to first grade. The teacher, alert to any incipient disturbance, called the child's mother, who in turn called us in panic. The teacher blamed Scotty's trouble on too much pressure for academic achievement at home. As clear indicators of such pressure, she pointed to his lack of interest in finger painting (which she interpreted as his being afraid of mess) and to his intense preoccupation with learning to read (which the school didn't encourage until age seven). We thought this diagnosis was suspect in the light of the youngster's happy progress at home and in nursery school up to the time of this school experience.

Looking back through Scotty's history, we found that he had been a quiet baby, hard to distract, and with a long attention span. He was highly sensitive to noise and never would lie in a soiled diaper. During his first summer he would coo all afternoon in his outdoor playpen while he watched familiar objects. His basic pattern expressed throughout infancy and continued through the preschool years was one of persistence, clear goal definition, and very low distractibility. In this he very much resembled Ellen, whom we described above. Once Scotty decided to do something, he persisted until he had reached his objective. If interrupted, he reacted with a tantrum.

He had an older brother, Bill, who spent a lot of time with him. Scotty, at four, had watched him do his homework and asked about the letters of the alphabet. He would sit patiently copying words under pictures Bill drew for him while the older boy did his lessons. He had been talking for months about going to first grade and learning to read like Billy. He was willing and able, but whenever he tried to read in first grade, the teacher insisted that he turn to a play activity instead. His reaction to this distraction and frustration was characteristic—a tantrum. The teacher, instead of analyzing Scotty's problem, dismissed it with a cliché: He is being pushed too hard at home by his overambitious parents. When the child was moved to a school that allowed him to learn reading in the first grade, his "deep-seated" problems disappeared. Of course, Scotty still has the problem of learning to direct his reactions to frustrations into more productive channels than temper tantrums, but this is another matter.

One mother we have known had failed to wean or toilet train her three-year-old daughter or even leave her alone with anyone else for an evening because she didn't "believe in making issues over the crucial steps in development."

When it was time for nursery school, the mother found that her daughter would have to be toilet trained to be accepted. Then the mother became panicky. She asked for help. When we talked about Joan's background, we found that her reaction pattern was characterized by irregularity, mild intensity, and easy adaptability. It seemed to us that, given these characteristics, if her mother had set a schedule for her, she would have been a model little citizen by three, rather than a whiny baby around whose demands the whole family revolved. It also appeared that she could still be readily trained by firm scheduling and consistent handling. The father agreed that Joan needed some rules, and her mother was desperate enough to be cooperative. By the time nursery school began the child was trained.

Since the mother was so worried about the traumatic effects of separation, we suggested that the father take Joan to school. The child was perfectly happy for two weeks. Then the mother decided to visit and see how well the child was doing. Joan then began to cry every morning when she left. At this point the father decreed that Joan should go on the school bus. She had a fine first year at school. Her problems and the family's would never have begun if her mother had been guided by Joan's characteristics rather than by theories about the dangers of growing up.

Because they are different, children won't all react well to one set of rules. A child who is highly distractible, with a short attention span and with moderately intense reactions to people and experiences, is not likely to do well in a school where there is no set routine and everyone walks around doing what he wants to from hour to hour. This setting doesn't bring out his individuality. It lets him drift. The more articulate, more positive, more intense children get the teacher's attention *and* the benefits of the freedom and richness of opportunity this kind of school offers.

Babies who eat and sleep by fits and starts will rarely set their own schedules by the age of twelve months. This may not matter when the mother is as casual about time schedules as her child. It works out very badly, we have found, when she is not so casual, has other obligations, and feels guilty about her impatience with her irregular offspring and her own failure ("Am I rejecting? Is that why he won't sleep?").

A baby who placidly looks out at the world and lets things happen to him can easily have his needs overlooked with the *laissez-*

faire approach. His protests when frustrated are mild and brief. If he has more vocal and assertive brothers and sisters around, he may be steam-rollered almost out of existence.

Any set of principles to help parents with child care can only be a compass and a guide and not a rigid blueprint or prescription. Consistency is important, but so is flexibility. A compass points the way to a goal and serves as a guide for consistent movement, but obstacles in the direct path often make temporary detours necessary. The parents' functioning will become disoriented if they do not maintain a consistent direction. But they will also have to be flexible in dealing with special circumstances and complications that always tend to arise. We hope that parents will view the rules and suggestions presented in the following chapters in this light, as a guide but not as a prescription to be followed blindly and rigidly.

5 TO BED IF NOT TO SLEEP

Kathy's father is a musician. He sleeps late, rehearses all day, gets home for a quick bite if he has a chance, and then hurries off again for 8:30 performances. He didn't like seeing his first baby only when she was asleep; so when Kathy was five months old, her schedule was arranged to suit her father's routine.

Within a week Kathy was waking at 10 A.M., rather than 6, and eating breakfast with her parents. Instead of going to sleep at 6:30 like most babies, she was just getting up from her afternoon nap at that hour. Then she had a bottle, played in her pen while her father played at Lincoln Center, and was ready for supper with him when he got home at 11 P.M. She went to bed peacefully at 11:30 and slept soundly until breakfast was ready.

There is nothing sacred about sleep routines. Nor is there any magic formula that dictates the amount of sleep any given baby needs for health and happiness.

Most babies will tell you plainly when they are not getting enough sleep. This is one of the things they communicate very early in life. And most babies are almost as agreeable as Kathy was about arranging their naps to suit the family's convenience.

In their first weeks, babies sleep most of the time. They awaken and cry when they're hungry. After they are fed they usually go back to sleep very quickly until they are ready for something more to eat. In some children the pattern of eating and sleeping may at first be varied and irregular from morning to night and from day to day. In others a regular rhythm of sleep and wakefulness is present almost from birth. But in almost all a rhythm gradually establishes itself. Three or four weeks after birth most babies sleep from three

50

to four hours at a time during the day and evening, are satisfied with five feedings a day, and sleep about six hours at night.

Some time between the third and sixth month, most babies peacefully abandon the night bottle, and many of them sleep or lie contentedly in bed from the time they're tucked in after supper until the household is stirring in the morning.

By the time they are a year old they may nap twice a day and sleep ten or twelve hours at night. At some point in their first five years they give up first one and then the other of these naps.

Parents these days don't show the concern their grandmothers did about whether their children are resting enough. They usually know that if their babies are gaining weight and are active, lively, alert, and reasonably agreeable, they are getting all the sleep they need. When their children are cross, whiny, rub their eyes a lot, or seem sick, parents generally see to it that their babies lead a quieter life and get more rest and sleep for a few days.

If a baby misses his nap one day because grandmother arrives for a visit, or goes to bed late one night because out-of-town guests pop in and want to play with him, few parents are worried.

Since most babies are adaptable, this relaxed approach is satisfactory. Many families gently ease their new babies on to a schedule that suits the family's convenience as Kathy's mother and her musician father did. And as a general rule this process takes place so smoothly that it is hard for the average parent to remember how it happened by the time the baby is a year old.

Sleep problems, however, can develop even with the regular and adaptable child. In their enthusiasm over a new baby, some parents pick him up whenever he peeps, play with him after he's been fed at night, wake him up for visitors and play some more. When the baby is five or six months old and some of the newness wears off, the parents want him to go to bed and go to sleep. When he cries in protest, they immediately think something's wrong. Usually he is merely suffering from a change in signals. He has gotten used to play before sleep and doesn't want to give it up.

Such was the case with Lenny. His father and mother both worked in television. They got home at 7:30 or later, and their first move was to get the baby out of bed. They played with Lenny while they had a drink, then put him in the carriage next to the table while they ate supper, cooing and talking to him whenever he lost interest in their conversation and began to fret. When they put him to bed at 9:30 he went peacefully to sleep.

By the time Lenny was eight months old, his dinner-table interruptions were louder and more insistent. He wasn't content to lie in the carriage. He wanted to be held or joggled while his parents ate. They began to tire of playing with him for three hours every night. They wanted to resume their social life, and Lenny was frankly a nuisance when guests came.

It took them several weeks to re-educate the baby about bedtime. He was an easygoing, adaptable fellow who would have adjusted easily to any reasonable schedule they had set. In his wholehearted fashion he had adapted to the stimulating evening companionship of his parents, and he was not ready to give it up without a fight. He screamed when they put him to bed after the first half hour of fun and games, and when he screamed his parents were intimidated. Like many mothers and fathers, they interpreted his normal protest as evidence of fear and trauma. They comforted him. When they put him back to bed and he screamed some more, they went back to him. As a result, he continued to cry each night. Finally they let him cry it out for several nights, and he gave up the battle, went peacefully to bed like any other child with a fairly regular sleeping cycle, and has been no trouble and shown no emotional ill effects since.

As long as most babies tend to be adaptive and regular like Lenny, and respond to consistent ways of being handled, it seems sensible for parents to accustom them at the start to the kind of routine that will be practical and convenient in the long run. If parents do not mind joggling or patting a baby to sleep, there is no harm in beginning that way. If this is going to become burdensome, or if they know they won't always be on hand at bedtime to joggle and pat, it is probably unwise to start the practice.

Parents who enjoy carrying out a lengthy bedtime ritual of singing and telling stories should feel no qualms about establishing this custom. But they should not then be surprised when their children enjoy their company and entertainment and try to stretch out the routine by asking for one more song, one more story, or one more kiss as they grow older and more responsive.

Often illness, discomfort in teething, or an unusual change in family routines creates temporary problems with normally easy, regular babies. When, for some reason, the baby's accustomed schedule is disrupted, he gets used to the change, and when his mother tries to get him back to his regular routine, he objects.

Annie, for example, was, in her mother's words, the "best" of her three children. She didn't have to be put on a schedule; she seemed to have been born on one. Right from the beginning she ate every four hours and slept or simply cooed the rest of the time. If her mother was busy helping an older brother with homework, Annie would wait as long as half an hour for her bottle after she woke, simply lying in her bassinet and watching her hands.

When she was three months old, she caught cold. Every night she cried because her nose was stopped up. Her mother held her, put drops in her nose, and played with her until the medicine had taken effect and Annie could breathe easily.

The cold lasted a week. But Annie kept on crying at night. Her mother thought she might still be uncomfortable, picked her up, comforted her, and put her back to bed. But the waking continued night after night. Finally her parents decided Annie had gotten used to the new routine. They didn't respond when she cried. She stopped crying after ten minutes and went to sleep. This happened two or three nights. Then she went back to her regular pattern of sleeping through.

Jane's behavior, on the other hand, was a clear response to her mother's overattentiveness. Jane was a three-year-old, charming, adaptive, and regular. Whenever the family schedule had to be shifted, her program could be rearranged with very little effort. Her mother was expecting a second child and prepared Jane carefully for the event and for her absence in the hospital. Everything went smoothly. Jane spoke to her mother on the phone every day about the new brother, and her grandmother reported that she was just as easy and cheerful as ever.

When Jane's mother came home, she was careful to explain that she was going to stay. To make Jane feel more secure, she urged her to call whenever she wanted anything, particularly when Jane heard her mother taking care of the baby during the night.

Three weeks later Jane's mother was dropping with fatigue.

Jane was calling whenever her mother got up to nurse the baby. Although she had never made such requests before, Jane now asked to be covered or taken to the toilet. She also woke up between the feedings. She was perfectly cheerful, enjoyed the visits, and went right back to sleep when they were over. During the day she was happy and contented.

Finally Jane's mother gave up and reprimanded the child. "You don't really need me when you call. Unless you do, I'm not going to answer you any more."

The next night Jane called once. "I have to go to the toilet. Wipe me." Her mother told her to wipe herself and go back to bed. Jane did. A few hours later she called again, asking to be covered. This time her mother said, "Don't call me again." From that night the child stopped calling. She was cheerful and happy as before, and there were no changes in her behavior during the day to indicate that her calling had been anything more than a simple response to the suggestion in her mother's homecoming speech that Jane might want her. She was an adaptive child, and she responded to the invitation to call. When her mother told her to stop, she got that message, too, and stopped calling. The problem would not have developed if the mother had not assumed that Jane would be disturbed by her absence and by her baby brother's arrival. Sometimes it is better not to anticipate trouble.

The "easy" baby we've been talking about can develop erratic sleeping habits when his parents set an undesirable routine for him or handle him inconsistently. His sleeping pattern may also be upset when his schedule is changed for one reason or another. Most parents, however, recognize this kind of problem for what it is and know how to deal with it easily. Sooner rather than later their children learn to go to bed on time, sleep soundly and wait for breakfast when they awake.

The "irregular" babies present different problems. They do not have an initial consistent rhythm and also experience great difficulty in learning when it is time to sleep and time to eat. It is much harder to fit them into the family's design for living.

The characteristics of the irregular child are fairly easy to recognize in the early weeks of life. He has an erratic appetite and inconsistent requirements for sleep. As a result, he sleeps at unpredictable times both day and night, and for longer intervals at some times than others with no apparent pattern in sleep periods from day to day.

Quite often his irregularity is also evident in other behavior. Not only does his appetite vary, but so, too, can his demand for food. Bowel elimination may often be irregular as well.

This irregularity is frequently associated with slow adaptability to any change in schedules. Obviously, a child with these characteristics is not the "good" baby of the mother's dreams. He is difficult enough at first, but may become impossible if he is not recognized and understood for what he is. If parents rigidly apply a rule of self-demand and do not establish routines for him, he can become more and more erratic. Caring for him can then occupy most of both parents' time and attention. This may lead to mutual recrimination, self-blame, and guilt, and finally create serious family problems revolving around the child. Often this situation develops without parents' realizing what's happening. Their reading in the child-care field makes them quite properly sensitive to the possible harm excessive frustration may create in infancy and early childhood, so that they almost always choose self-demand scheduling. Unfortunately, when this doesn't work, they often become anxious and fearful of the possible consequences of instituting the consistent scheduling an irregular child may need.

Such was the case with Debbie. Her parents had studied the principles of self-demand before she was born and interpreted them as a rule to feed the baby whenever she showed discomfort. The baby books were reassuring and promised that as the child's digestive processes matured, she would settle into her own normal physiological rhythm of hunger and satisfaction, of sleep and wakefulness. Debbie was fed or otherwise attended to faithfully each time she fussed, but when she got to be six weeks old, there was still no sign of regularity in either eating or sleeping.

Indoctrinated to believe that a truly contented baby never cries and that good parents have babies who are always contented, the parents rushed to pacify her whenever she cried. The baby woke them three or four times a night. When she was picked up, she would coo contentedly while mother or father walked the floor with her. When put back in her crib, she sometimes went to sleep for a while; sometimes she fussed until played with some more. The parents could not even have a meal undisturbed. Debbie usually woke up crying sometime during the dinner hour.

The parents' response to the child's crying was not producing the promised results: a happy, noncrying child with regular patterns. Instead, it was creating a weary and irritable pair whose originally joyous view of parenthood was rapidly becoming jaundiced. If Debbie's parents had accepted the fact that she was a temperamentally irregular individual, they might have been able to train her to a sensible schedule early in life.

During the first weeks, some irregularity in the sleep and hunger pattern can be expected. When the infant awakens crying, food should be offered, even though he has been fed only an hour or two before. However, when the first weeks have passed with no spontaneous establishment of a well-defined rhythm, parents should begin to impose some regularity. This may be done by allowing three and a half or four hours to pass between feedings, or by not picking the child up during defined rest periods. With this regime, mothers must expect crying at first and be willing to tolerate it. The amount of protest will vary, depending on whether the baby is intense and persistent or mild and nonpersistent. Ordinarily, in several days or a week a rhythm is imposed, and feeding by the clock becomes easier. There may still be considerable amounts of irregularity in the amount of food the child takes from one feeding to another, but a more practicable routine will have been established.

The parents will probably not be able to alter the amount or timing of the irregular baby's sleep. This irregularity does the baby no harm. But they can modify his behavior when awake at night so that the parents can get the sleep they need. The choice lies between having a child who cries when he is awake unless he is being held or a child who may awaken several times during the night, but spends his waking time gurgling to himself.

Of course, most children who awaken because they are ill will cry from discomfort. They deserve and should receive attention. However, when he is no longer ill, the irregular child will frequently retain the pattern of crying for attention unless his parents consciously act to re-establish the desired routine.

When the baby is between six weeks and three months old, the parents can decide which of the night or early morning awakenings are to be treated as feeding times. On other wakings, after making sure that the child is well and does not need changing, they can ignore his fussing. If the baby is a persistent, nonadaptive, and intense child, they should be prepared for a loud and prolonged protest. If he is adaptable, mild, and nonpersistent, they can expect the crying to be gentle and brief.

Most vigorous children will resist efforts at change. The protest, however, should not be interpreted as *prima facie* evidence of emotional trauma. There is no evidence that making demands as such on children creates serious and persistent problems. On the contrary, it seems to make life easier for the irregular and slowly adapting child to learn in gradual stages to live according to family rules, if the lessons are reasonable, and the teacher is reasonably flexible. As the child gets older, his difficulties in adjusting to changing situations and new experiences seem to diminish. By the time he is in first grade, he usually has learned to get along almost as easily as the child who was considered "easy" from the start.

Alice, for example, had been very like Debbie in her early months of life. Her parents had weathered the irregularities of her sleep-wake cycle by taking turns getting up with her, and also by refraining from playing with her every time she woke. They had gotten used to hearing her cooing and talking to herself at odd times during the night throughout her first years. They noticed that whenever there was any change in their living arrangements, Alice reacted by becoming irregular in her sleeping pattern. They were appropriately responsive. On a weekend visit, when Alice was three, she wakened throughout the night just as she did at home. But in the strange surroundings, she would not stay in bed but popped out of the room ten or more times during the evening, or came out and crawled into her parents' bed sometime during the night. Her father and mother had learned that she took time to get used to new things. Rather than avoid visits away from home with her, they deliberately continued their pattern of life. As a result, by the time Alice was five, visiting was no longer a strange experience, and she stayed in bed even during her wakeful periods.

Many educated parents tend to be oversensitive to the possible symbolic emotional significance of any negative behavior in their children. They may have read that disturbance in sleep is often a symptom of deeper trouble. If a child cries at bedtime, they want to be sure he is not anxious. If he wakes up in the night, they are worried about nightmares. If he has a bad dream one night, they search their hearts and the child's past experience for possible clues to the upset. They forget that all children have some disappointments, hurts, and shocks, some irregularity in their normal behavior, and that variety in sleeping habits is so great that almost any behavior in itself may be normal.

Mothers who have several children distinguish between one child's sleeping pattern and another's. One infant wakes up at the slightest noise, while another sleeps through a thunderstorm or a boisterous party. One baby stirs at a glow, while another is oblivious even if a light falls directly on his face. There are infants who can be awakened for company and go peacefully back to sleep when the visit is ended; others will stay awake for hours, seemingly ready to start a new day. One baby awakens from his nap instantaneously, full of smiles and gurgles; another usually wakes up cranky and whiny for a half hour or more—he almost seems to need his morning coffee!

Teething and minor illness affect children's normal habits differently. Billy's sleep is interrupted by a cold and stuffed nose, but when it clears up he goes right back to sleeping through the night. With another child, like Annie, described earlier, it will take several days before she stops crying for mother to pick her up when she wakes.

Betty's behavior varies according to who comes when she calls. If her mother responds, she goes right back to sleep. If it's her father, she makes a series of requests, each of which he patiently grants. Only when mother takes over and tells Betty firmly to go back to sleep does she give up.

The move to his summer home won't change Larry's dependable bedtime routine one bit. Amy, however, will spend the first week in the summer cottage fighting sleep and calling regularly to find out where everyone is and what he is doing.

The specific effect of unusual circumstances in his life on each child's sleeping pattern reflects his own individuality. However, a marked variation from the child's own norm in sleeping behavior may be a sign that deeper emotional troubles exist. The parent who knows his child well should have no trouble telling the difference between random upsets in sleeping that reflect his usual way of reacting to change, illness, or other new experiences, and a basically modified behavior pattern that may signify real trouble.

It should be recognized that emotional problems rarely show up in sleep disturbance alone. The child who won't go to bed, can't sleep, or wakes up often in the night complaining usually shows other evidence of unhappiness and fear. Perhaps he won't go to nursery school. Perhaps he can't play with other children or even join their games as a silent participant.

A child who has been growing more independent by moving away from his mother to play with other children may change and cling to his mother's side. A youngster who had never sucked his thumb may begin to keep it in his mouth as a permanent fixture or begin to chew perpetually on his collar. He may begin to stutter, develop a tic, or show a pattern of wild and disorganized running around that is unlike him. He may start hitting out at other children or grabbing their toys for no apparent reason. The change in his sleeping pattern is associated with one or more other alterations in his behavior. These changes may show fear directly, or they may be inappropriate ways of acting which the child uses to disguise his fear. An attempt at bravado, for instance, may cover up apprehension and anxiety. The disturbed behavior usually continues and increases and stands in the way of his becoming "older." This kind of situation should be discussed with a trained diagnostician of children's emotional problems.

With the exception of such problem situations, children can be trained to sleep when it is convenient for the rest of the family. This is best accomplished by parents who are aware of the child's individual temperament and handle him in a manner that is sensitive and consistently appropriate.

Tears are not to be confused with trauma. Children will protest what they don't like, whether it is isolation from family fun, a change in bedroom, a move, or a return to routine after illness has brought them unaccustomed extra attention. Most parents learn when to wipe away tears and offer sympathy, and also when to adopt the firm tone of voice that means business. A mother won't necessarily expect even the best six-month-old baby to go to bed in a new place without a fuss. Nor would she enforce a change in schedule when she knows her child is not feeling well or has been having more than his share of disappointments or upsets.

Sensitivity to the child's temperament and consistent handling, while always important, are particularly vital in training the irregular baby. Even babies who don't need much sleep will adjust to scheduled rest periods during which they play quietly without disturbing the rest of the household. And they can be taught to go to bed peacefully at a regular time even if they don't go to sleep. Irregular children may take longer to meet family requirements, but with patient, consistent handling they also adapt.

6 BREAST OR BOTTLE?

The popular tendency to treat every new report about child care as if it were scientific gospel is dramatically illustrated in the breast-versus-bottle controversy.

Until the 1920's there was no reliable, safe, and adequate substitute for breast milk. Infants fed on cow's or goat's milk all too frequently developed dysentery, tuberculosis, or severe summer diarrheas. With the development of knowledge of germ diseases and their control it became possible to prevent bacterial contamination of cow's milk, and refrigeration enabled it to be stored safely. Advances in the science of nutrition made it possible to modify cow's milk so that it would duplicate mother's milk in essential food elements.

When these scientific advances led to the perfection of formula feeding, breast feeding among most American middle-class mothers became quickly obsolete. By 1930, the mother who nursed her baby might be classed with the woman who still baked her own bread and wore clothes made from her own homespun wool. The nursing staffs in New York hospitals treated the insistent breast-feeder as a kind of crank. Prevailing opinion viewed the practice as a slightly unsanitary nuisance.

The advent of safe and adequate formula feeding came at a time when women were moving out of the home in increasing numbers into higher education, jobs, and political and community activity. Naturally enough, many women enthusiastically welcomed this new method of feeding which did not require their almost constant attendance on the baby at home.

But with the next wave of enlightenment breast feeding came

back into favor almost as fast as it had been deposed. In the post-Freudian epoch, word got around that healthy child development was dependent on a close physical, emotional, and spatial relationship between mother and child. The young infant was said to require sensory stimulation as well as emotional contact with its mother on a continuous basis. These presumed needs were even called "the rights of infants."

Breast feeding was one very important part of such a relationship. It was asserted that the mother who nursed her baby gave it not only milk but also the physical love and stimulation it needed. The mother who chose the bottle or, even worse, had no milk was considered unnatural. "Unnatural" was a euphemism for "bad." There was widespread agreement among those who did the talking and writing in child-care circles that a woman who really *wanted* a child would automatically be able to nourish it with the equipment nature supplies.

Bolstering the trend toward breast feeding, both the medical literature and the mass media have carried frequent reports on the value, if not the virtual necessity, of the natural way for healthy child development.

Thus, a widely read professor of sociology asserted in a 1961 article in the *American Journal of Psychiatry* that breast feeding "should continue for at least nine months." He called this one of the "indispensably necessary conditions for the wellbeing and healthy development of the infant. Any culture which discourages its mothers from behaving in this manner is likely to contribute in a major way to the predisposition to mental illness in its members." [1]

The discovery of safe formula feeding was a landmark. For the first time in history it offered the mother a choice. She could still elect to stay home and nurse her baby if her own milk supply was adequate. But now she could also go out to work knowing that her baby had safe and nutritious milk available in the formula. There was now also a healthy supply of milk for those babies whose mothers couldn't nurse them and didn't have wet nurses.

Unfortunately, psychological theory has served to eliminate this freedom of choice by turning the issue into another proving ground for testing the mother's essential femininity. Thus, if a woman wants to work and have her baby make do on bottles while she's gone, she is a "rejecting mother." If she has no milk, she wasn't made for motherhood. If she dislikes the notion of nursing her young, she's psychoneurotic or latently homosexual. If her nipples are the wrong size, shape, or texture, or if her baby is uninterested in her breast, she has betrayed her true colors; she is not really womanly. She will never measure up, and her child will suffer the consequences.

But is it true that breast feeding is always the best?

From our experience and a review of available evidence, the categorical advocacy of breast feeding for every mother is unwarranted. There is no scientific support for the view that it is always the preferred method of feeding. In fact, the findings from our own longitudinal study show no difference in the frequency of behavior problems between babies who have been breast fed and those who have been nurtured on cow's milk.

This question has also been studied by Martin I. Heinstein, now Research Psychologist for the Bureau of Maternal and Child Health, California Department of Public Health. Reviewing the experience of ninety-four children from the University of California Guidance Study who have been observed from birth to age eighteen, he finds no evidence "that breast feeding as such provides a psychologically better start for the child," and "no indications . . . that supported the older notion that there are advantages for the physical health of the child in breast rather than formula feeding." [2]

An interesting experiment was conducted some years ago by a research group at the University of Iowa. With the mothers' permission, normal newborn infants whose mothers' labor and delivery were uneventful were divided into three groups. Ten were put on breast feeding and ten on bottles. Another ten were cup fed from the start. [3]

In line with psychoanalytic theory, the authors of the study should have seen evidence of frustration in the cup-fed babies. All the babies were closely observed to see how much sucking they did on bedclothes and on their fingers. The investigators regularly touched the infants' lips with a finger to determine variations in the strength and speed of their sucking reflexes. The children were also watched for restlessness as expressed in body activity.

The behavior of the cup-fed babies was indistinguishable from that of the others. They showed no stronger sucking response when they were stimulated by a finger. They did no more sucking on fingers or bedclothes, and they were not measurably more restless than the other babies studied.

Advocates of the emotional values of breast feeding frequently say that studies of this sort are of no importance because they deal only with early life and therefore fail to explore the long-term consequences of oral deprivation. While the authors of the Iowa study never did a follow-up, an interesting check on this very question has been made quite by chance. Not long ago a Kansas City psychiatrist heard of a fourteen-year-old child (not under treatment) who had been a patient of the pediatrician whose advocacy of cup feeding from birth had provided the impetus for the Iowa group's study. Through the boy's mother, the psychiatrist was able to find twenty former patients of this doctor, all of whom had been cup fed from birth. He paired them for cultural and economic background with classmates who had been breast or bottle fed. All the children were then interviewed and given personality inventory tests by psychologists who did not know how any had been fed in the first three months of life. When the interviews were analyzed and the test results sorted, no statistical difference could be found between any of the groups. Bottle fed, breast fed, and cup fed were indistinguishable in terms of emotional development and adjustment.[4]

It is apparent to mothers, pediatricians, and baby nurses that there are great variations in sucking activity among babies from the moment of birth. Some babies *seem* to find their thumbs at once and suck despite unlimited nursing. Some have to be taught to suck by having milk expressed into their mouths. Some won't use a pacifier at all. In our opinion, most of the variations in the sucking activity in babies basically reflect a given child's behavioral and temperamental type.

It seems high time for mothers to enjoy the luxury of being able to choose between breast and bottle feeding, secure in the knowledge that the best way is what fits their needs and the baby's.

There are all sorts of reasons why a mother would want to nurse her baby: because the idea appeals to her; because she's compulsive about housework and likes the thought of *having* to sit down and do nothing for fifteen or twenty minutes while the baby's at the breast; because she has so much milk so fast it seems the easiest thing to do.

There are all sorts of reasons for giving a baby a bottle: because the mother doesn't like breast feeding; because she doesn't want to or can't be tied down to the baby's feeding schedule; because she's afraid she won't have enough milk.

There are many good reasons, too, for *abandoning* breast feeding early in life. Some babies don't adapt to the mother's breast or nipple; the shape of their mouths and the shape of mother's breast don't fit together. As a result, the baby is often frustrated and the mother feels inadequate. This may threaten parent-child relations.

Some mothers have to wait several days for the milk supply to come in and may find this period of waiting difficult. They get upset worrying if they will be able to nurse. This threatens their milk supply completely. They feel guilty and unmotherly. They shouldn't. If they can't nurse, they should just turn to a formula.

There have been many pronouncements about feeding in recent years, and most of them, like the pronouncements about breast feeding, are more ritualistic than rational. At one point pediatricians were issuing rigid regulations about how much sucking time a baby was to have each day, with warnings about the emotional consequence of not sucking enough. We have seen lusty babies screaming with frustration at feedings because their mothers had made the nipple hole so small, to drag out the sucking time to the prescribed length, that the children couldn't satisfy their hunger fast enough. Such commandments were issued in total disregard for the differences in sucking activity, appetite, and intensity of reaction between babies.

There have been many, many critical comments about the practice of feeding babies from propped bottles, on the theory that babies fed in this impersonal way would suffer the effects of maternal deprivation. One wonders, however, what else the young mother with a hungry baby should do when she has to stop feeding the baby to settle a quarrel between her other two children, fix a scraped knee, answer the door, get lunch for the other children, or simply sit down and look at the paper for a moment. Such advice seems to us to be predicated on the belief that mother love can be created by following written instructions and dispensed at prescribed ceremonies. Often the effort to mother by formula, when the formula is uncongenial, makes for awkwardness and guilt and interferes with any spontaneous affection that might develop between mother and child.

As long as a baby's health and safety are not in jeopardy, there is no more need for a mother to disregard her own nature and ways of doing things than there would be for her to ignore her child's temperament in taking care of him.

7 FEEDING WITHOUT FUSS

By the time a mother has a second child, she has stopped being a slave to rules about feeding—if she ever was one. Experience has given her the courage of her common-sense convictions. She adapts the menu and timing of each child's meals to his particular needs and habits, and acknowledges and respects some of his peculiarities, trying to temper them so that they don't inconvenience the rest of the family. She has found that children can grow normally and enjoy food without eating exactly when, what, or how much the rules prescribe.

A new mother, however, may feel that her baby's very life depends on how well she follows the latest and best advice about feeding. Pediatricians say mothers of first babies ask more questions about feeding than about anything else.

A new mother may want to know what to do when her baby has gone to sleep leaving half of his bottle. She may be upset because he still screams with hunger after his bottle is empty. She may be seriously concerned because he won't drink orange juice or eat Pablum, or because he doesn't like solid foods. She often worries needlessly because the baby fails to follow the rules of the child-care book, the pediatrician, or even the next-door neighbor in one way or another. She hasn't had practice enough to realize that rules are for guidance only and almost invariably need to be adjusted to suit the child.

For most mothers, the initial jittery uncertainty is short lived. Feeding the newborn is not as simple as it may have been when babies were breast fed as a matter of course, but it is much easier than it was in the early days of artificial feeding. In addition to elaborate procedures for safeguarding the baby from bacteria, parents were held to rigid rules for amounts and timing of meals. The formula was supposed to be measured precisely to make sure that it would duplicate mother's milk as closely as possible in calories and nutritional composition, and even in temperature. Parents were told that failure to follow instructions about sterilization and schedules exactly could result in anything from a fatal infant diarrhea, milk anemia, or rickets to just plain bad eating habits.

Like many customs that later became outmoded, the feeding practices that prevailed before the 1930's made sense when they were conceived. Many babies did die from infant diarrhea before milk was properly pasteurized and refrigerated. Many babies did suffer from deficiency diseases such as milk anemia and deforming rickets. So it was important to be extremely careful about sterilizing babies' food properly, and it was wise to add the prescribed solid foods to the diet at the prescribed time.

In that era it took hours to prepare a baby's diet for the day. A spoonful of freshly scraped meat might take a half hour to get ready; a dish of cereal might take an hour to cook. When a baby turned up his nose at his food, mothers were not only panic-stricken about the consequences for his health, but frustrated because they had worked so hard preparing the meal.

Today a wide variety of safe, ready-to-serve foods for babies (including premixed formulas) is available everywhere in the country. A great deal of research has settled the nutritional needs of babies from birth on. We know that all sorts of variations in formula, diet, and schedule will not seriously affect the baby's progress.

Mothers' attitudes toward feeding reflect the changing scene. Why worry whether Junior eats his carrots when there's a substitute he might like in the next jar on the shelf? Why get into a dither if he doesn't want his meal at all, since it took only a minute to prepare, and we know that he can skip several meals without suffering?

Pediatricians and baby-care books have encouraged this relaxed approach, which is all to the good. Fixed feeding formulas and schedules are no longer advocated. Approximate directions for quantities and kinds of foods that all babies should get at various ages are suggested as a very rough guide. When, how, and how much of this or that a baby should actually consume each day is left largely up to mother. She is usually told to use her baby as a guide. Frequently she is given a blanket rule: Feed him when he cries.

Self-demand is actually not the innovation it seems. During the many centuries of human history when breast feeding was the rule, mothers fed their children routinely when they cried and took them off the breast when they stopped sucking, sometimes two minutes, sometimes twenty minutes, later.

Feeding on demand still works well with the large majority of babies who develop fairly regular appetites and hunger cycles in the first few weeks, especially when they are easily adaptable. By the time they are four to eight weeks old they get hungry about every four hours. When the needs of parents or other children require some shift, the regular, adaptable baby can usually be fed or put to bed earlier or later without much fuss.

With the irregular child, however, the situation is very different. If he is left to his own devices, his mother can never be sure when he will be hungry from one feeding to the next. He may go two hours between feedings at one time and five hours at another. Some overconscientious mothers try so hard to follow the self-demand approach with the irregular child that they find themselves occupied around the clock trying to satisfy him, with little or no time for their husbands, their older children, or their other activities.

There is no evidence that self-demand is harmful for the irregular infant, but because it is so hard on the rest of the family, it is often best to modify or even give it up with such a child. However, before deciding to put a child on a regular schedule, parents should be prepared to hold to it once they start. The mother may allow a half-hour leeway with feeding time if the baby is crying fiercely or sleeping soundly, but not much more.

Some irregular babies adapt quickly to a regular routine, once it is set. Others continue to be more or less erratic about hunger and sleep. But even if they continue to fuss and cry for an hour before feeding, there is no cause for worry. We found that these babies usually fuss just as much on self-demand as they do on a schedule.

We remember one baby whose mother was feeding him every

hour around the clock during his first week home from the hospital. She wanted to do the "right thing," which she understood to be self-demand. At the end of the week, we persuaded her to try a sechedule for the sake of the rest of the family and promised her the baby would continue to thrive after the first noisy adjustment. She took a deep breath and agreed to feed him every four hours. For the first twenty-four hours the baby fussed or bellowed almost constantly. Halfway through the second day he was fussing very much less, and he was hungry enough at the end of a four-hour wait to drain his bottle. By the fourth day he had settled peacefully into an imposed routine, and his mother decided he really should have a chance to decide for himself again. She fed him when he began to fuss—three hours after a feeding. The next time he fussed two hours later, and by the end of the day the feeding routine was right back in bedlam.

The schedule was quickly resumed. The second time it was easier for the baby to adapt to it. After several days our friend felt confident enough to feed the child a half-hour ahead of time. But she never again let down the bars more than that.

How can you tell when a baby is crying because he's hungry? How can you tell when he's full? How do you know when he *really* doesn't like a particular food?

To the mother fresh home from the hospital with her first baby these vital questions may seem unanswerable. Six months later the same mother probably won't even remember that she had these worries. Most babies themselves are reliable guides on questions pertaining to early feeding.

While the great majority of babies have fairly regular hunger cycles, they have different ways of signaling that their stomachs are empty, depending on their individual temperaments. The intense and active infant wakes up screaming and kicking with hunger and then sucks with gusto until he is full. The less active, mild child may lie quietly and only whimper slightly. His sucking will be businesslike and quiet.

The milder and more adaptable he is, the less forceful he will be about letting his mother know when he's had enough. The lusty, intense baby who screams for food and drains his bottle quickly will usually make himself just as clear when he's full. Some babies of this kind will clamp their lips tightly when they've finished. Some will kick and scream. But the quiet, mild baby may just doze off, letting the milk dribble out of his mouth.

Mothers get a chance to see how their babies react to new experiences when they start giving other foods: fruits, vegetables, meats, cereals, juices. The way a baby takes his Pablum may tell a great deal about how he'll adjust to other changes in his routine. Will he take it right off? How intense will his acceptance or refusal be? If he rejects the new food how long will it take him before he accepts it? Will he react the same way to each new taste? Or will he have selective reactions, eagerly accepting and savoring some foods and rejecting others just as clearly?

During the first months, when much of a mother's time with the baby is spent in feeding him, she will find answers to all these and many more questions: how active, how intense, how adaptable, how persistent, how easily distracted, how positive he is, and so on. The answers will give her clues to many facets of his temperament.

The conditions of modern life and the generally flexible prevailing attitudes toward bringing up children combine to prevent the kind of feeding problems that used to be common. This has been strikingly evident in our study. Many of the parents have consulted us with regard to all kinds of problem behavior in the children, but only in a few cases has feeding been brought up as an area of concern. The few serious feeding problems we have seen represented symptoms of more generally maladjusted relations between parent and child.

The minor problems that occur around feeding are straightened out quickly and easily in most cases. The babies who do not get hungry regularly or have the same appetite from meal to meal, who do not give clear signals when they have had enough or do not respond in definite pro or con fashion to new foods, may require some modification of feeding routines.

The child who doesn't stop when he's had enough may eat too much. He will vomit or gain too much weight, and his mother can take the hint and put him on a measured diet.

The baby who dozes off before he's had enough will wake up hungry an hour later. When this happens often enough, his mother can feed him less at a time but more frequently, or find simple ways to keep him awake and sucking until he finishes his bottle at each feeding.

The child who refuses everything new at first may be discouraging to his mother, but she usually learns quickly to keep offering tastes of new foods regularly until he takes at least some of them. This kind of baby who doesn't like *anything* new really needs to be encouraged to broaden his diet and eat some of the things he refuses at first. He may be perfectly well nourished on milk and a very limited selection of foods that he will accept. But his *laissez-faire* approach to his diet does not necessarily work to his advantage in the long run. In fact, he seems to need as much early experience as he can get in learning to adapt to new ways, new foods, and new places in infancy in order to be able to make later adjustments to the new easier. (See Chapter 13.)

We don't for a minute recommend making mealtime a proving ground where the question of whose will is stronger—mother's or baby's—is tested. This should never become the issue. We do recommend that mothers continually offer children of set ways little dashes of new foods on the end of a spoon, even if they wriggle, writhe, and shudder at most of them. They may accept a few or none during their first year, but they gradually learn to try new foods with this encouragement, just as they gradually learn to enjoy more people, places, and experiences, when they are repeatedly exposed to them in early life, without being forced to do anything more at first than sit and look.

All children can develop sudden likes and dislikes. A baby or a toddler of two goes on a food binge. He may want bananas at every meal. He may cry for more potatoes and refuse all other food until he gets them. He may also suddenly and violently (if he's the intense type) reject a food he's liked. Today mothers can afford to be amused by such shows of caprice. It is so easy to find a substitute for any rejected food on the baby-food shelf of the supermarket.

All babies—or almost all—reach a point when they want to feed themselves. Trouble may start right here if the mother interferes because her baby is making a mess or taking too long. Many mothers who complain that their three-year-olds have to be spoon fed turn out to have sternly and consistently discouraged their children's first efforts at self-help.

The not very persistent baby will give up if his mother won't let him try. The intense, persistent baby will fight to feed himself. If he happens to have the same kind of determined mother, mealtime becomes chaotic. The battles between mother and child affect the child's appetite: the child stops eating; the mother starts pushing; the child persistently refuses; and so on.

Even though many mothers find it much easier to manage feedings themselves, it is better not to interfere with the child who wants to hold his bottle at eight months or spoon his own Pablum at a year. It will mean more mess to clean up and slower mealtimes, but the inconvenience may be worth the ultimate reward. We recommend a large bib, a spread of newspapers on the floor, and a spoon for the baby, so small that it cannot make much mess.

Most babies have a decline in appetite when they are going on two. Tussles over eating often begin at this time.

Through the first two years children grow faster than at any other time. A baby who weighed six pounds at birth can easily weigh thirty pounds at two. To achieve this tremendous growth he requires prodigious quantities of nourishment. But between the ages of one and a half and two, his weight gain tapers off. Instead of putting on eight ounces a week, he may gain less than eight ounces a month. His appetite falls off accordingly. Mothers who don't realize this sometimes worry. Once they worry, they may push food. Obviously they often run into resistance. Trouble can be avoided if one remembers that the two-year-old is normally a much smaller eater for his size than the young baby.

Mothers who are normally casual about whether a child misses a meal now and then may become anxious when a *sick* child won't eat. They feel that, once the acute phase of illness is past, the child will regain his normal strength and vigor faster if he eats heartily. Of course, he hasn't been active and he isn't hungry, and mother's efforts to pile on the calories may make him even less eager to eat. If the child adjusts to new ways quickly, he will expect her coaxing, cajoling, and entertainment with his meals to continue long after he has recovered his normal appetite.

All children, in fact, prefer being entertained, whenever possible. The mother who tries to use television, stories, songs, or games to divert a child who doesn't like to eat will find that when the child gets to be two, he wants to look at television while he eats and drags out every meal interminably.

There is nothing wrong with distracting a baby if it makes life simpler. But one must be willing to go on distracting him, even when he might normally be able to feed himself, or stop making mealtimes a three-ring circus long enough for him to learn that he must feed himself if he wants to eat. When children don't feed themselves between the ages of two and three, it is often because their mothers help them one day, leave them alone the next, go back to helping on the following day, and so on, in erratic fashion. The message usually has to be consistent to be learned. It is wiser for a mother to start babies off with methods that she will find easier to continue.

The food faddist—the child who will eat only peanut butter or cream cheese—is usually made in infancy. He may have been a child who didn't like new things, and his mother may never have given him a second chance at food he rejected; or he may have been a persistent child whose mother believed in making things he didn't want. Both these types of children might learn to broaden their repertory of food if they were given enough opportunities to try new things in peaceful surroundings.

Problems in feeding, rare as they are these days, generally develop from a mother's or a grandmother's anxiety about a baby's getting enough to eat, plus failure to use consistent methods of training. It should help to remember that babies almost never need to be coaxed or coerced. They will eat when they are hungry, if they are not fed too often. Some need more food than others; some need it more often than others. But one child's method of eating is as good as the next one's, provided his health is good and his weight gain appropriate. He may be slender or stocky, short or tall, and use up more or less energy, according to size, stature, and the amount of moving around he does. The energy he burns up, rather than any innate superiority or flaw, determines how hungry he is and how much food he wants from meal to meal.

8 GRADUATING TO THE CUP

When Roger was eight months old, he reached out for his five-year-old sister's cup of milk at the breakfast table. She helped him hold it while he tried to drink. The first few sips dribbled down his chin and onto his bib, but Roger managed the next few more successfully. Then he seemed satisfied and took up his bottle again. Daily he reached for his sister's glass. As time went on he took more from the glass and less from the bottle. Finally, when he was ten months old, he pushed away his bottle, crying and flailing his arms around whenever his mother came anywhere near him with it. When she gave him a partly filled cup, he reached out for it and drank eagerly. Roger's mother continued for weeks to coax him to take a bottle again, but he remained immune to persuasion.

Forty years ago this mother's attempt to keep her baby on a bottle would have been regarded with unalloyed horror. In those days mothers were frequently advised to break their babies' bottles when the children were ten months old. Prolonged sucking was supposed to keep babies babyish beyond their time.

Roger's mother, in striking contrast, was afraid that weaning her baby too soon would cause emotional insecurity which might lead to thumb-sucking in childhood and possibly neurotic overdependence in adult life. Fearful of what the other mothers at the playground might think if they saw Roger drinking from a cup, she took a bottle with her each day. When her son wouldn't suck, she simply put it away. Not until her child was over a year old did he get his cup in public.

Although few mothers would interfere so strongly with a baby's efforts to wean himself, most of those we have talked with would agree with Roger's mother that weaning is a very ticklish business. Their attitude derives principally from the Freudian view that when a child is weaned before he has fully experienced the pleasure possibilities of sucking and passed on to the next stage in ego development (the anal), he may be permanently arrested at the oral level emotionally. Deprived of the gratifications appropriate to his age, this reasoning goes, he would ever afterward unconsciously hark back to the frustration. His early scarring would show up in overdependence, an insatiable need for love, and little ability to give love to others.

It is doubtful that Freud ever expected his theories to be so literally applied. At any rate, observation of the children in our study offers nothing at all to substantiate such views. On the contrary, everything we have found points to the fact that weaning is as uneventful a stage in human development as it is in the maturing of all mammals.

Weaning appears as a hazard only if one subscribes to the theory of instinctual oral sucking drives which cause trouble if they are frustrated. If sucking represents such a developmental need, as the advocates of late weaning hold, children fed by cup or weaned to a cup at an early age would suck their thumbs more than children fed by breast or bottle and weaned later. The thumb-sucking should occur, according to the theory, as a substitute gratification for the loss of nipple-sucking. No such relationship has been discovered in any systematic study.

Observation of babies indicates that for most of them weaning, far from being frustrating, is actually a satisfying accomplishment. The child who drinks from a cup can set his own pace. He can sip, gulp, drink steadily or intermittently; he has much more control than when he has to suck through the small holes of a nipple. One additional step has been taken in mastering his environment.

In addition, the baby who is weaned can feel more grown-up. He now does one more thing the same way his parents and older brothers and sisters do.

The age at which children are ready to be weaned varies, as does the age at which they are ready to walk and talk. Some babies make all changes more quickly and easily than others without being in any way brighter, emotionally superior, or more advanced.

When a baby can be weaned also depends on his environment. Roger might not have been so insistent about the cup at eight months if his sister had been only two instead of five, and therefore unable to give him a hand. He might not have thought of the cup at all if he had no older sister or brother. He might not have succeeded if his mother had been worried about spilling and had refused to let his sister offer him her cup. And last but not least, he would not have wanted the cup if he had been the kind of child who is relatively slow in muscular development and coordination. Such a baby probably would not have been at the breakfast table at all at eight months of age. If he had been, he certainly would have been uninterested in a cup.

At the other extreme from Roger is Jimmy, a boy of four and a half. To his mother's dismay, he insists on sucking his bottle while he watches his favorite television shows every night. But this child is no more a demonstration of the toddler's extensive needs for sucking than Roger. He simply illustrates the fact that entrenched habits are hard to dislodge.

His mother accepted what she had read: Babies give up the bottle when they're ready and shouldn't be hurried. When Jimmy was a year old, he wiggled so much that he was hard to dress. When he had his trusty bottle, he was quiet. When his mother put him down for his nap, he got up, but when she gave him a bottle, it seemed to put him to sleep and she could take a nap herself. At the age of two Jimmy would wake up at night, and it was easy to get him back to sleep with a bottle. When the child was three, his mother began to think it was time to quit, but decided to wait until Jimmy was better adjusted to his one-and-a-half-year-old sister. Besides, the bottles in the early morning gave her a little more time to sleep.

A year later Jimmy still had his bottle, and his mother was worried that it signified some emotional problem. It never occurred to her that he insisted on bottles because she had found it more convenient not to wean him.

There was no question in our minds that four-and-a-half-year-old Jimmy could have managed a cup easily during his second year if he had been consistently encouraged. He learned to dress himself easily and quickly when he was three and his mother was busy with his baby sister. This was his way of tackling all new lessons. Like Roger, who discarded his bottle before he was a year old, Jimmy was reacting in his individual way to his particular environment rather than demonstrating the inexhaustible sucking needs of all children.

In our study, about two hundred children already have been weaned or have weaned themselves at ages ranging from ten months to five years. We have seen no indication in any of them that weaning was frustrating or deprived them of instinctual pleasure-seeking needs. Whether children abandoned the bottle at ten months or five years did not influence the amount they protested, or the whining, clinging, fears, general fussiness, or sleep disturbance they showed. One age may be as good as another to begin the weaning process if the mother is not too much in a hurry and takes her cues from the child.

Most of the infants in the study who were weaned early made it more or less on their own. They were usually imitating an older brother or sister.

Mothers in our study were fairly easygoing about the whole thing. They expected their babies might want the reassurance of a familiar bottle at night for some time, even after they were drinking from a cup regularly during the day. If a child cried for his bottle and refused the cup during an illness or upset, the mothers didn't take a "cup-or-nothing" stand. They also recognized that any period when the child was adjusting to other new experiences or a change in routines was not the best moment to take him away from the bottle.

It seemed to be just as easy to wean most babies quickly as quite gradually. The most easily and quickly weaned babies were those who were most adaptable, well coordinated, and positive in their initial responses. These are the children who tend to investigate new things, whether a new toy or first spoon of Pablum, with immediate interest. Often such children began drinking from a cup without anyone's even noticing how it happened. The fairly pliable child also appeared to be easy to wean.

As far as weaning is concerned, the problem child was likely to be the unadaptive, negative, poorly coordinated baby. Even this kind of baby, however, got along without too much trouble when his mother had a clear idea of what she wanted to accomplish, stuck to her plan consistently, and was not thrown by temporary setbacks.

By the time such a baby is old enough to wean, his mother usually knows him well enough to anticipate the way he will react and makes her plans accordingly. When she intends to train her baby to drink from a cup, she will be prepared for a period of fussing for the bottle. The period will vary according to the persistence of the child.

The mother of a difficult baby will pick her time carefully, but once she has started she will carry on persistently. Sometimes it may help to explain to the child what is going to happen and give him a few weeks to get used to the idea. But once the change has been started, consistency is almost imperative. If the bottle is withheld for several days, then given when the child fusses a great deal, then taken away again, and once again restored, the parent may in fact be teaching the child that if he fusses a little bit longer, the weaning will be abandoned.

The evidence from our study group of youngsters is that there is no one "best" age for the child to be weaned. Therefore, the family's convenience and the general health and welfare of the baby should be the decisive factors

Weaning before two is perfectly possible and permissible. Weaning before one, however, is usually more trouble than it's worth, since the level of muscular coordination is not yet developed enough in most children to make cup feeding convenient for either mother or baby. But any child who weans himself before he is a year old means business and should not be interfered with. When this happens, the baby probably has precocious muscular development, plus an older brother or sister he wants to imitate.

If there is a special reason for weaning a child early, there is no reason to fear harmful consequences, provided the change is made without too much fuss and furor.

Most middle-class American families wait until after the second birthday, and frequently close to the third, before weaning. It is very little trouble to pour whole milk into a bottle for the baby, so it doesn't make much difference to a mother to have a child wait this long to be weaned. Two or three, then, might be a fairly good age to aim at.

Weaning has been advertised in some contemporary child-care circles as capable of causing a great array of temporary and far-reaching developmental and personality problems in children. As a result, many mothers have been understandably apprehensive about teaching their children to drink from a cup. Anxiety has often made them wavering and inconsistent in handling the change-over. In the confusion, some babies who don't adjust easily anyway have developed problems that need never have occurred. With a matter-of-fact approach, dictated by the baby's temperament and needs, few children have trouble making the change.

9 THE END OF DIAPERS

Many mothers approach toilet training gingerly. They are told that it must not be attempted too early or too late, that it must not be too forced or too permissive. Cautioned against making toilet training the focus of parent-child duels, they are simultaneously advised that battles cannot be avoided. No wonder mothers are often convinced of trouble before they start.

It seems incredible that a task accomplished routinely in most of the civilized and uncivilized world for a very long time could create so much worry in twentieth-century Americans. That it does is a tribute to the influence of Freudian thinking on the field of child development.

Here are a few typical remarks from the professional literature:

"Some of the hardest lessons [for the child] center around toilet training." [1]

"Training is difficult . . . it arouses strong emotions—perhaps as strong as are ever evoked in the child again. Anger, defiance, stubbornness, and fear all appear in the course of such training. . . . A child may get the impression that it is pursued by an all-seeing, punishing guardian." [2]

"Bowel and bladder training has become the most obviously disturbing item of child training in wide circles of our society." [3]

These grim pronouncements are based on the Freudian theory that toilet training inevitably frustrates the child's instinctual pleasure in bowel activity (the anal drive). Frustration, according to this view, may permanently disturb the personality unless the training is carried out with the utmost caution and skill.

Specifically, psychoanalytic teaching says that the child looks upon his feces as a valued possession. He may feel deprived of this treasure if he is asked to have a bowel movement in the toilet. To avoid making a child feel robbed, toilet training should aim at persuasion rather than direction. The goal is to make the child give his possession to his mother as a gift in order to win her approval.

If the child struggles against being put on the toilet seat, he is presumably expressing anxiety about giving away his gift and is thus undecided about the *value* of his mother's approval. On the other hand, if he sits without struggling, but later has his bowel movement in his diaper, he is seen as winning a battle with his mother through sabotage. If he accepts the new procedure, there may be a question about whether he feels coerced and beaten down.

This theory never suggests that toilet training may in fact be a practical next step in growing up. The whole matter is approached as if the sole actor were the mother, and the child's behavior merely a reflection of the mother's handling. The mother is often made to feel that her status as a mother depends on her success or failure in toilet training.

From the evidence we have gathered on the children in our study, we can find no reason at all for continuing to assume that toilet training involves painful frustration or a struggle with the mother for mastery. By observing the children from early infancy, we have gathered detailed information on their functioning before, during, and after training. We found few instances of disturbance —less than 5 per cent of the group. The few children who seemed upset to any significant extent were also having difficulties in many other areas. The toilet-training difficulty was only one of a number of symptoms resulting from general problems of psychological development.

More impressive than the almost total absence of toilet-training problems was our discovery that many children seemed eager to be trained and showed great pride in mastering this big step in growing up.

Some children, whose mothers were fearful of training them too soon, actually trained themselves by imitating an older brother, sister, or friend. A few mothers tried to conceal this fact, so fearful were they of criticism for not following the experts' warning against premature training.

Since children differ greatly in their reactions and temperamental characteristics, it is impossible to find one rule for toilet training that will work for all. How can the parent deal with the individual differences that influence children's reactions to being trained?

Some infants can be trained to use a potty regularly by the age of nine or ten months without any trouble. Others may not be trained easily until they are about two and a half years old. The infant who can be trained early is one who has a regular bowel movement at a predictable time every day. He is a quiet child, who doesn't mind sitting still. If he is put on a potty seat just before his usual time, he will almost always have his movement there. Even if it is really his mother and not he who is trained at this point, if she makes a habit of putting him on the potty regularly, it will become a habit for the baby to perform regularly within several weeks or months. Eventually he will begin to call his mother if she does not seat him in time.

Other children, however, may not be trained until they are two and a half years old. They are generally youngsters whose bowel movements have always been irregular. There is no specific hour each day when a mother can learn to put such a child on the potty to build an association between the bowel movement and the potty seat. If he happens to be a physically active child who resists sitting still under any circumstances, there will indeed be a battle to keep him on the toilet for any length of time for a purpose he cannot understand. The mother may think the battle is over toilet training, but to the infant it may be only a struggle against restraint. In this case, putting him on the toilet seat teaches him to associate the seat with imprisonment. It does not train him to have his bowel movement there.

Figuring out the kind of baby she has is no great mystery for the new mother. She changes his diapers from the time he is born and therefore knows quite well how regular his bowel movements are and how difficult it is for him to stay still. If he is an active, irregular child, his toilet training had best be left until he is old enough to know what toilets are for. He can then identify their use with growing up and gaining mastery of the environment.

Even though the regular child can be trained in his first or second year, there is no reason for a mother to feel compelled to train him early. Convenience should be the guide. Good laundry and diaper services have certainly made it a good deal easier to delay toilet training. Often a mother's household schedule or her vacation plans may decide the issue. If she cannot put the baby on the seat at his regular daily time for an unbroken stretch of several weeks, she had best postpone the effort. Since unfamiliar surroundings may make toilet training more difficult for some children, a mother may do well to postpone training until a vacation trip or an out-of-town visit is over.

Do all regular babies get trained without incident? Certainly not. Often a mother will introduce her baby to the toilet at his usual time for having a bowel movement. He will sit without fuss, then have his movement after he is back in the diaper. Mothers who have read a great deal about training may quickly assume that the baby is defying them. This is not necessarily true. Before drawing such an inference, one would have to answer several questions about the child.

Is he the kind of infant who develops very strong habits and shows discomfort when a routine is changed? If his mealtime is shifted, does he eat poorly? If his bath is given in a different tub or at a different time of day, does he make a fuss? If he is this kind of one-track baby, he may have a very strong association between his bowel movement and the warmth and texture of the diaper. Sitting on the hard and possibly cold toilet seat could inhibit his intestinal function and make his sphincter clamp tight.

There would be nothing willful or hostile about his resistance. It would be purely physiological. The mother might do well to keep up the potty procedure for a week or two to see whether the baby gets accustomed to it. If he does not, she should stop trying for several weeks or months and then start again. The important thing is for her to understand that this is not a defeat for her or a victory for the child, but simply an indication that this particular child needs to be older before he can be helped to comply.

Often the best time to make the second attempt with children whose training has been postponed for one reason or another is when language has developed and the situation can be discussed with them. At the age of two and a half or three, the irregular child, for example, may see a friend or older cousin use the toilet for bowel movements and try to learn in order to identify with this grown-up behavior. He can then be asked to try to notice when his stomach feels funny and urged to go to the toilet himself. If this doesn't work, his mother might ask him to tell her as soon as he has had a bowel movement in his diaper. If he does not follow this simple request, assuming of course that he understands it, the mother has the choice of postponing training again or making a disciplinary issue out of this request. The child who persists in ignoring the bowel movement in his pants might be punished in the same way that he would be punished for refusing to stop kicking the seat in front of him in a bus or for having a tantrum in a store when he was denied a toy: by removal from the pleasurable activity. For example, if he were playing outside with a friend when he failed to tell his mother about the bowel movement, he would have to leave his playmate and play alone for an hour or so. Such measures, though they may appear drastic, are occasionally necessary to make the child pay attention to his mother's request. This routine could be observed consistently until the child learns to follow instructions. Once he understands that bowel movements should be made on the toilet seat, the rest of toilet training usually goes quickly.

After the irregular child is trained, the mother might let one slip-up pass now and then. However, when more frequent accidents go unnoticed, the child may revert to his earlier behavior. In such instances, the training process may have to be repeated, though it can be expected to go quickly.

The children we have been talking about up to now are not real problems. There are children, however, who do present special difficulties in toilet training. Some have actual physical disturbances that interfere with training. The child who is constipated and has hard bowel movements may find elimination difficult and even painful at times. Until this condition is corrected, he will have trouble fulfilling the demand that he use the toilet. He may withhold his bowel movements to avoid pain. Toilet training should be delayed until the physical problem is solved.

The child with a tendency to bouts of diarrhea may also be puzzling for the mother who is trying to train him. Just as things seem to be working out, diarrhea interferes with the program, and the mother may have to wait several weeks before starting all over again. This, too, is essentially a pediatric problem, and toilet training had best wait until it is cleared up.

Other children are management problems on many fronts. They may have sleeping problems and eating problems as well as being difficult to train. With them the issue is not toilet training, but the whole parent-child relationship. Sometimes the management problems are the result of obvious psychological disturbances in the mother which may interfere with her ability to handle her child properly. But a more common reason is that an overpermissive mother has made little or no attempt to regulate the child's life, on the assumption that he would regulate himself when he was ready.

Some infants *do* regulate themselves. Others on this regime simply stay unregulated. Until the mother's concept of parenthood changes, they will remain unchanged. For example, the child may be an active youngster who cries when he is restricted. If the mother sees her role as keeping him from crying at all costs, she will never leave him on the toilet long enough to perform. Such a mother would not hesitate to take a sharply pointed pencil away from him despite his crying, but she interprets routines differently. If her child cries because his play period is ended and he is put to bed, she assumes that she is doing him harm. She reacts similarly if he cries when he is put on the potty. For such a parent, toilet training is only one of many training problems.

Speculations about her underlying conflicts over "motherhood" or "femininity" are unnecessary. Such theorizing merely produces new confusion and distress. It is much simpler all around for her to revise her approach to toilet training by noting the specific characteristics of her own child and adapting the training procedures to fit his reactions. She will find the problem less formidable when she forgets the gloomy warnings about what she may be doing to her child's "fragile psyche" and deals with toilet training as a quite ordinary fact of life that requires, above all, a matter-of-fact approach.

10 ESTABLISHING HOUSE RULES

Parents today seem to have more trouble with discipline than with anything else. They complain that their children just don't mind. They don't mind their fathers and mothers. They don't mind their teachers. They can't follow the rules.

Investigation often discloses that the child has never actually been taught to obey. As a result he may have a disregard for rules, orders, and authority. The parents who are responsible for such signs of anarchy among the young are not, as one might expect, always neglectful, indifferent, casual fathers and mothers. They are often intellectually sophisticated men and women who take their responsibilities to their children seriously. While they may not always recognize it, they have deliberately failed to instill discipline in their homes. Convinced that the only safe way to adult mental health is through free expression of instincts and drives in childhood, such parents have conscientiously refrained from imposing authority, setting limits, or demanding consistent compliance.

Fifteen years ago the well-behaved child was frequently regarded as the mark of a bad parent. The obedient little boy was assumed to have been cudgeled into this behavior by a cruel and domineering parent.

Although this extreme attitude has changed somewhat, in our clinical experience, many educated fathers and mothers still appear to be quite confused about the purpose and wisdom of teaching children to mind.

Recent pronouncements on discipline have stressed the fact that children "need limits," but what the limits should be and how firm the parent's stand in setting them and enforcing them are moot questions.

Fathers and mothers are perfectly secure about preventing children from putting their hands in the fire, playing with matches, electric plugs, poison, and running off the sidewalk into oncoming traffic. Even the most recalcitrant children seem able to abide by family rules where safety is involved without suffering any permanent traumatic results or deep-seated conflicts. But outside the definite and clear-cut rules about safety, chaos often reigns.

Mother wants to put out the light and say good night to Jimmy, but Jimmy, two and a half, whines for one more story.

Mother says, "No, Jimmy. You've had a story. Mommy has to get dinner."

Jimmy whines. "Just one more." This time his chin trembles.

"Tomorrow we'll have another."

Jimmy sobs loudly.

Mother worries about the effect of his going to bed unhappy. She gets a book and says: "I'll read just a *short* story," as if she were not *really* countermanding her first decision. Jimmy smiles happily until the story is over, then begs for another. His mother finally *does* leave him crying anyhow, and also totally confused about what she really means and expects.

Parents are afraid to make their children unhappy. Therefore they often try to establish discipline without tears or sullenness or even any verbal protest.

Another kind of discipline problem: Jimmy's father and mother have dinner guests. Jimmy has been told he may pass the crackers during the cocktail hour. Jimmy passes the crackers once, twice, a dozen times. Finally Jimmy's mother recognizes that Jimmy is as much the center of attention as if he were doing handstands on the coffee table. Her guests are tired of saying, "No, thank you," with impeccable restraint. No one can talk. Mother takes Jimmy to bed. He screams. She feels guilty because she is putting him to bed for her own convenience. She gives him another chance and tells him to sit still.

After several more fetchings and haulings, Jimmy finally is put to bed by his father, both screaming. The guests are subdued. The party is a flop because Jimmy's mother couldn't bear to be "selfish" enough to think of herself before her child. Many people have the mistaken idea that human rights apply only to the young. They feel that it is inexcusably immature for adults to expect children to accede to their wishes or even their quite essential needs.

Before children's confusion about minding is straightened out, parents have to clear up their own ideas about what discipline is. Many parents, and even some child-care experts, tend to think of discipline only in negative terms. They recall with a shudder the nineteenth-century slogans: "Spare the rod and spoil the child" and "A child's will has to be broken."

This kind of discipline is certainly bad. It may turn a child into an intimidated, inhibited individual or a rebellious, impulsive one. But this does not mean that the parents' only alternative is an absence of discipline, a *laissez-faire,* overpermissive approach.

On the contrary, discipline can and should be a positive learning experience for the child. The question should not be how much or how little to "spoil" him or "break" his will. Rather it should be how to help each child learn the rules of social behavior in a way that is best for his individual temperamental style.

When a child learns safety rules, learns what is good behavior with his parents and other grownups, learns not to break or damage furnishings and books, all these accomplishments can give him a sense of achievement. He will have taken another big step in growing up, in becoming more like his parents and older brother and sister, in being trusted to do all kinds of things without constant supervision. Learning the rules, then, brings an advance toward greater freedom and more mastery of the environment. It is not a battle for control between parent and child, but a rewarding challenge.

Parents sometimes lose their bearings with discipline because they are afraid to frustrate the child. Actually, there is no evidence to support the notion that frustration as such, even when it evokes obvious displeasure, need create emotional problems in children.

Frustration frequently accompanies all kinds of learning experiences. When an infant first tries to walk and tumbles, when he first tries to drink from a cup and spills the milk all over himself, when he first tries to tie his shoelaces and gets them in a knot, when he first tries to ride a bike and falls, he may get very frustrated. In these situations parents are clear that frustration is an unavoidable but not harmful side effect of this learning process.

Learning to mind is much the same kind of experience, and the benefits are often just as important. The refusal of a child's spontaneous wishes or the restraint of an activity may cause frustration. However, the goal is not to frustrate the child, but to make it easier for him to get along in the world.

The first disciplinary measures are usually instituted to safeguard the child. In addition, parents want their children to learn their own beliefs and standards. Discipline—setting down what is and is not permitted—helps teach children these standards. Very early in life, parents also begin to make children aware of the conventions and standards of the community so that they will be able to get along comfortably when they begin to move out of the family circle.

General principles in teaching rules and standards are of some value but must be individualized, just as in teaching a child to ride a bicycle or to read. Certain conditions and methods do seem to make things easier for all children.

The child learns faster when directions are clear. When Tommy runs away from mother and darts out into the busy city street, the mother loses no time in stopping him and making clear by word and, if necessary, by the reinforcement of a sound slap that such conduct is completely out because it's dangerous.

Limits in other areas should be established just as plainly. Of course, if the issue is not as urgent or imperative as it is with regard to avoiding danger, physical emphasis is not necessary or even desirable. The degree of forcefulness of emphasis should be related to the importance of the issue. But in all cases the rule must be expressed with clarity and consistency.

If mother wants Sally, aged one and a half, to start learning to keep hands off the family's books, she must say, "No," and be ready to remove the child from the books if this doesn't work. Distracting Sally or talking about *why* she shouldn't touch the books may help, but neither approach is a substitute for the simple message: "No."

Inflexible rigidity, except for imperative reasons of safety, is of course not desirable. Although consistency is the cornerstone of sound discipline, common sense will dictate times when bedtime rules should be modified or table manners relaxed.

It is easier to be consistent about rules and easier to teach them when there are not too many. Parents and children alike find it hard to remember endlessly refined requirements for table conduct, bedtime ritual, care of possessions, and behavior in public places. There comes a point of diminishing returns, when more and more demands on a child produce less and less response.

Lessons in discipline are essentially like other learning experiences of the child. He is not expected to learn to walk or to tie his shoes the first time he tries. Parents realize that the child learns a little at a time, and sometimes, when he is tired, he forgets what he seemed to have mastered the day before. When a toddler takes his first step, the whole family will applaud and give him a hug. He joins in the enthusiasm and tries again. When he falls, he looks quickly around to see whether his friends are still with him. Of course they are. They cheer him on to keep trying. They don't scold him for failing to repeat his accomplishment. They expect him to make mistakes. The same should apply to a child who is learning to mind. Encouragement and rewards generally are more effective than harsh criticism for failure and constant, nagging pressure to do things right.

It may be laboring the obvious to remind parents of the immense reservoir of good will toward life and the world that most babies seem to possess. They want to learn, to grow, to act like grownups they know and love. They want to be taken along, included in the family's activities, and then in their class activities. When they find that what they're doing pleases the people they want to please, they try to remember to behave that way. When daddy hoists Sally overhead and says, "Big girl," the first time she puts her blocks away without a reminder, she is encouraged to greater efforts at obedience. When a child who likes to cut is told, "If you carry the scissors right, I can let you use them," he will want to try. Positive reinforcement always seems more effective than the same amount of criticism for omissions or disobedience.

Of course, even general principles must be applied differently to different children. The capacity to learn rules and follow them varies from child to child as much as the capacity to learn to talk. Some children learn to obey very quickly; others must try over and over again and be told the rules repeatedly. As in many other areas of training, knowing the child's ways and his style of learning makes teaching easier. One child, learning to walk, gets up in his crib, tumbles, gets up and tumbles, and repeats this again and again, beaming and smiling in spite of his apparent lack of progress. When his mother comes in unexpectedly, he claps his hands, jabbers in excitement, and exhibits his new activity with obvious pleasure and pride. Another child goes through the same routine, shrieking and screaming in distress, but he too does not stop struggling.

A third child may practice in secret. He can be heard from the next room, pulling himself up in his crib, then bumping down again, but when anyone goes in to look at him, he stops short as if embarrassed to be seen. Still another child may not experiment at all. He may simply get up and walk one day as if he had been at it for months.

Some children trail around the room, moving from chair to table to mother's skirts. Others push a toy around, apparently under the illusion that the toy is holding them up instead of the other way around. Others experiment with balance and steps on their own, but as soon as their mothers appear, they hold up their hands to be carried with a cranky, imperious, "Up, up."

The way a child learns to walk is usually the way he learns other things, including the rules of social living. We have found this to be true as we have followed the development of children in our study. "It was never necessary to lay down rules," one mother said. "Dianne never did anything she wasn't supposed to." With a little questioning, we found that Dianne's parents really *had* told her not to run across the street or touch red-hot irons, and had explained why. The same was true with other rules she seemed to follow automatically. But she obeyed so easily and quickly that her father and mother couldn't remember how it happened.

Dianne not only learned the rules easily. She was adaptable in every way, perfectly comfortable going along with whatever the order of the day might be. When she was only a year old her mother sat her on the floor in front of her first Christmas tree. The child's eyes opened wide at the beauty of the glass bulbs and fascinating twinkling lights. But her mother had only to say: "Mustn't touch," point to the tree, and Dianne sat quietly, content to look while her mother went back to her cooking.

She was not timid. She splashed in the waves the first time she was taken to the seashore. She gurgled with delight the higher her father pushed the swing. She joined the three-year-olds with a brief good-bye kiss and no backward looks for mother on her first day at nursery school. She was simply an adaptable child with definite, positive responses to most new experiences.

Tommy illustrates another kind of child's reaction to rules and restrictions. "He argues every point," his mother told us. "But once he realizes that there's no way out, he will not only follow the rules but make sure that all the rest of us do, too."

Tommy's way of learning the rules was characteristic of all of his adjustments to new ways. It was hard for him to adapt. He seemed to be acutely uncomfortable doing anything new. He showed this quality during his first bath when he was a week old by screaming and arching his back and turning red. He showed it by refusing his first spoonful of Pablum with almost as violent a reaction. As Tommy grew older, however, his parents began to realize that he always quieted down in the end. After many, many baths he settled down long enough to discover that the water was fun. After many, many rejected dishes of Pablum, he began to relish it. After protesting against going to bed for a year and a half, he finally went peacefully *if* he had *all* of his toys. In fact, he protested only when his bedtime was delayed too long. He was persistent in resisting change, and then persistent in sticking to the change once he had accepted it.

Teaching Tommy to observe even the most basic safety rules was a formidable task. Firm restraint, which Tommy's repeated transgressions provoked, only brought on tantrums. Explanations that Dianne understood and followed at once seemed to be invitations for him to go on doing as he pleased.

As a two-year-old, he would rush for the big slide as soon as his mother sat down to read. Before she could stop him, he'd be teetering on the top step. Stern admonitions seemed to make him run away faster the moment he was set free. Finally, after his mother had repeated the prohibition over and over, and taken him down from the slide time and time again, he learned to stay down on his own. Tommy learned to mind just as he had learned to eat. Each new rule provoked immediate rebellion. Slow, persistent, firm, patient repetition of the demand finally brought obedience.

When he was four he reached the point where he repeated his rules for his playmates and saw that they followed them: "Mustn't go near the edge of the platform," or "That's *my* toy. I'll give you a turn later." By recognizing Tommy's limited capacity to make quick shifts in behavior, his mother had kept him on her side. His quality of persistence became an asset instead of a hindrance. If she had been impatient, too demanding, inflexible, she would have intensified his negative and oppositional reactions. If, on the other hand, she had been inconsistent and vacillating, retreating from her demands when he objected loudly, Tommy would have learned that his mother would give in if he cried long enough.

The success of Tommy's training was also greatly helped by his mother's positive approach. Learning rules was not only the firm, patient repetition of "No" and "You mustn't." Tommy's final adaptation to a rule was praised by his mother and rewarded. When the child finally learned to sit quietly in the car, his mother said, "That's fine. Now we can trust you in the car. We can now take you on a trip to the zoo." When Tommy began to obey the safety rules for crossing the street, he was told, "You're really growing up. Now you can cross the street to visit your friend Joey." (Though his mother did watch from the window to make sure he didn't backslide.) These rewards made the little boy pay more attention to other directions he got from his parents.

Ruth was rather like Tommy, but her parents were different. They didn't have the capacity to ride out her frequent storms of protest. Her mother was not consistent, sometimes being ultrafirm or almost cruel. The child would get just *one* chance to play in the park sandbox. If she grabbed a toy from a playmate and ran off with it teasingly, her mother would lift her out brusquely and wheel her home, strapped into her stroller and screaming, and then dump her in her crib and slam the door. Next day the same incident might occur, but this time the mother would quietly remove the toy, give it back to the playmate, and let Ruth cry out her disappointment.

Ruth's father was not inconsistent. He simply washed his hands of her, convinced she was "out to get us." This made her teasing refusal to mind worse. She seemed to believe this was the only way to get attention. Her father's response was to walk out of the house or to spank his three-year-old daughter and put her where she couldn't bother him. Instead of learning to mind, Ruth became whiny and negative, as well as unadaptable.

Is a child who seems to adopt the mores of her family and later of her community almost by osmosis necessarily happier or more valuable than the child who has trouble learning the rules of living? Of course not. He may be a more convenient child to have around, because he doesn't make any trouble for anyone, but he can very easily be lost in the shuffle. Because such a child is quiet and adaptable, parents can easily overlook his wishes, and even his needs, in the rush of other family business. Busy parents may almost forget that he's there. The noisy demands of a more assertive, harder-to-please child may drown him out. The parents may not notice his quiet, unassuming resignation to being neglected. Sometimes, almost by oversight, parents impose many more restrictions and demands on the adaptable child than they would on a protesting youngster. It is important to pay special attention to the "easy" child's desires, even though they may be expressed so quietly and tentatively and modestly that they are sometimes hard to hear.

Noisier, more demanding, less compliant children have a harder time learning limits, but they have the same will to please, the same appreciation of praise and reward, the same need for approval and companionship that all children have.

The less adaptable child will respond to his parents' efforts to maintain friendly relations with him. In handling such a child, it is a good idea to teach only one thing at a time, and to be scrupulously consistent and patient. The parent should simplify demands and prohibitions, and emphasize expressions of approval.

The parent of a less adaptable child may need a mental list of issues to work on. First on the list would come rules that must always be followed. These might include restrictions against lighting matches or poking at electric sockets. At the bottom of the list would come rules that it would be nice to have observed, but are not really important enough to stir up a storm. An example would be a rule about going to bed the first time the child is asked. Other requirements might be shelved temporarily in order to avoid a situation in which the child's every move seemed to be evoking parental displeasure.

The very expressive child and the quiet one may have equal depths of feeling, which may be judged only by the persistence of their reactions. The enthusiasms of the child who shrieks with joy may die quickly. The poker-face child may sustain interest much longer. Some children will make a major fuss when they have to stop something they like. Five minutes later, if left to weather the crisis, they may have forgotten the episode and be happily engaged in something else. Mildly expressive children, on the other hand, may yield easily and show by apathy or grave silence that they still are brooding over the deprivation an hour later. The opposite may also be true. A very expressive child may also feel deeply, and a quite child may not always be nursing intense inner feelings. "Still water" sometimes, but not always, "runs deep." Therefore, judging the importance of any restraint or deprivation only by the volume of a child's reaction may lead parents astray.

No matter how sensitive parents are to a child's temperament and his day-to-day capacity to conform to their standards, there are bound to be times when gentle measures do not work. At such times, many parents shy away from punishing a youngster because they are afraid to make him "unhappy." But for many children, especially the slow adapters, punishment is at times the only way to get across the idea that disobedience has to end.

There are several guidelines for making punishment work and keeping it to a minimum. Punishment should not be used to "show who's boss" or to let off steam, but to underscore the necessity for minding. This goal can be accomplished if the punishment grows out of the specific issue. It should fit the crime and not be unrelated to it. For example, if a three-year-old persists in crossing the street when he's allowed to play outdoors alone, his mother might make him play inside for a day.

A child who keeps throwing sand in the sandbox might be taken straight home every time he starts to do this.

A child who won't get out of the tub when told to would have to forgo his bedtime book because he had used up the time for it. The child who makes a scene in the market when mother won't buy candy might be left in the car next time.

Punishment should be appropriate. If a mother flies off the handle every time the child veers from model behavior, he can't judge what's important and what isn't. His mother's reactions are his only signal about how to behave, particularly in the years before he can talk well.

Is it right to spank? There are occasions when a whack, administered with dramatic suddenness, accomplishes what weeks of patient and repeated restraint have failed to do. It is most effective when administered with calm determination and a brief, clear reminder of what it is for: "I said no. I mean it." When a child can't keep his hands off sharp objects, stay out of the street, or refrain from hitting his three-month-old brother, spanking is often a helpful deterrent.

But though punishment is sometimes necessary and effective, it should be considered a last-resort measure. If efforts to control a child's behavior are a constant preoccupation of the family, something is very wrong. Even the most negative, hyperactive, intense, independent individual is agreeable some of the time.

When things don't go well, parents might ask themselves these questions:

1. Are we making too many demands at once?

2. Are we expecting more than this child at this age and under these circumstances can deliver? For example, one mother of a very active three-year-old expected him to play quietly alone with blocks for half an hour at a time. When we suggested that she interrupt him and change his activity every fifteen minutes, she found that he could comply.

3. Is discipline clear? Hitting a child and screaming, "I told you never to strike Timmy," is not guaranteed to discourage hitting. Confusion comes also from giving in and handing a child candy after having refused this through a fifteen-minute supermarket tour punctuated by repeated whining requests. Such episodes only teach a child that whining pays.

4. Are we gaining compliance by constant bullying, bribing,

screaming, and hitting? Such tactics teach children to obey only those whom they can't outsmart or overcome. It may teach them, incidentally, to bully the weak

5. Are directions so overloaded with "reasonable" explanations that the command is not clear? More than one child has to listen to a long discussion of why it would "be better for us to stay home from the party because then we would not be so tired tomorrow when we are going to the circus, unless we would rather go to the party than to the circus, and we could if we had not already bought the tickets for the circus, so don't we want to tell Jimmy we can't come this time?" The child may well answer: "Tell me what you want me to do." Sometimes too much explanation obscures the simple fact that you are *telling* a child what to do.

6. Do we both agree about what's required of the child? Do we support, rather than undermine, each other in general? When the father tells Jimmy he must stay home from grandmother's because he doesn't know how to act in the car, mother must not reverse the order. Some children learn to follow each parent's separate demands. Others become confused and stop following both.

7. Are we keeping the child's individual temperament in mind in planning our approach? If two-year-old Kenny is persistent and slow to adapt, don't expect him to give up poking at electric outlets after one or two "no's." If Karen is highly active, don't expect her to sit quietly all through a long car ride. Break the trip up and give her a chance to run around with each stop.

One last reminder. Discipline is much simpler when it's viewed as natural, necessary, and helpful to the child as well as the family. Children are very durable and very human. So are parents. Both make mistakes. When tired, worried, or angry over completely unrelated matters, parents may violate every one of the many principles discussed here. Sometimes they can admit they're wrong; sometimes they don't need to. Children reflect the continuing, prevailing attitudes and actions of fathers and mothers. They have an even greater capacity than their parents to forgive and forget single incidents.

11 A CODE OF CONDUCT

Three childen, aged five to eleven, arrived with their parents for a country visit. The youngsters rushed into the house, ignoring the greetings of their hosts, and fanned out like beagles inspecting a new kennel. They went through all the rooms, pulling out toys, books, magazines and dropping them whenever something else caught their fancy. Sometimes two of the children went for the same thing at once. Screaming, pummeling, they fought over the prize, occasionally destroying it in the struggle. At lunch the oldest announced to his mother, "You know we don't eat soup," and left the table. When peanut butter was substituted, all three took their sandwiches and continued their prowl, leaving a trail of crumbs and grease spots.

By nightfall the visitors had destroyed one doll, most of the pieces of a Monopoly game (thrown in the fire by one of them during a losing streak), and an elaborate block city that had been under construction for weeks (knocked down by the five-year-old because there was no more ice cream).

At bedtime the hosts' oldest child complained in tears, "It isn't fair. They're ruining everything."

His mother could only agree that the guests were pretty fiendish. She promised that they would never be invited again.

But their bad behavior was not their fault. Their mother had brought them up on the theory that children learn good manners spontaneously by example, that they treat other people kindly when they feel kindly, that they feel kindly when they are happy, and that they are happy when they are loved and not frustrated.

Actually, their mother did have clear standards of behavior and manners for herself. She did believe that good table manners, consideration for others, and politeness were important. When one of her children was rude or inconsiderate or messy and noisy at dinner, she winced and even blushed for shame. But she kept controlling the impulse to criticize and to demand better manners from her children. She kept reminding herself of what she had read and been told, that such demands might frustrate and inhibit her children, that if she saw to it that they were happy and secure they would learn good manners by themselves.

As the incident of the country visit suggests, the theory doesn't always work.

Some adaptable children, as we have explained in Chapter 10, learn to fit in so easily that parents, looking back, can hardly remember when they first walked, talked, slept through the night, or were toilet trained.

This kind of child will usually imitate his parents. When his father and mother are gentle, soft-spoken, and considerate, he will follow suit. No one has to tell him to say "Please" or "Thank you." He passes the cookies, automatically it seems, before taking a handful for himself. He shares without thinking and takes turns with his toys.

Being so adaptable, he picks up bad manners just as easily as good ones, when he begins to move out of the family circle. If he has a friend who calls his grandmother a stinker, he may do the same next time his grandmother comes to visit. If his parents' manners are for public display, rather than private consumption, he's apt to miss cues and give the private version in public: "This meal is lousy" at the neighbors' house or "You talk too much" when Uncle Joe comes to dinner.

Most children, however, don't absorb manners, good *or* bad, in this effortless way. They learn them just as they learn to read, by being taught. Those who are not taught, like the unfortunate trio described above, often suffer as much as children who aren't taught to read.

Manners are part of the mechanics of our civilization. Children need manners to help them find their way with other people. Manners not only make it easier for them to get along; they also encourage awareness of the world outside.

The child who has no manners is one who has never become conscious of anyone else or anyone else's needs. This is usually even sadder for him than for those he offends. His behavior keeps him from getting a chance to play with other children and to make friends. It may finally stunt his healthy personality growth much more than that bugaboo of modern parents, harsh frustration.

Some parents don't teach manners because they think such teaching makes children too compliant. The polite child, according to this thesis, is a conformist who goes with the crowd. Actually, the opposite usually follows. A traveler in a strange land needs to know where the roads go before he can decide which one to take. The child must learn the social customs of society before he can judge when to observe and when to ignore them. A child who doesn't know how to behave is apt to follow the leader blindly. When he knows his way, he can choose freely what's best or sensible for him.

Manners are not taught simply to smooth the way for a child socially. They reflect family values. When, for example, parents tell the toddler, "Don't push, spit, scratch, kick, hit," they are telling him that they disapprove of getting what you want or of settling arguments by overpowering someone else.

Children should be clear that language and behavior which is acceptable for their agemates may not be appropriate with grownups. Rules of good manners with their elders should be spelled out for them. Rules for behavior with grownups—"You can call your friends 'stinker', but it is rude to talk to me that way" or "Let the lady out of the elevator first, Tommy"—are not formulated only to help make a child socially acceptable, but to teach him to respect and defer to those who must be his guides, in his early years at least.

Much of the behavior that parents expect reflects their attitudes toward other people. When a little girl on the bus asks, "Why does that woman have the black thing on her eye?" the mother replies quietly, "She may have something wrong with her eye. Don't talk about it. It might make her feel bad."

Some parents rebuke their children when they are very young for making fun of other children for being poor, odd-looking, or of an unfamiliar ethnic group. This is to make children understand that their parents want them to judge people for what they are; that they disapprove of name-calling or making oneself feel bigger by making someone else feel smaller.

Manners also express taste. They vary from family to family almost as much as home decoration does. One family doesn't allow children to chew gum, another does. One mother doesn't allow patent-leather shoes for school, another doesn't care. One family insists on a boy's wearing a clean shirt for dinner, while the next doesn't even notice whether the youngster has brushed his hair for the family meal.

Manners vary with environment. Once in a while one meets a five-year-old New Yorker who bows and scrapes, saying, "Please" and "Thank you" and "Don't mention it" as easily as a courtier. While you can't help admiring his mastery of decorum, you also wonder when too many manners become as burdensome as no manners at all. The Little Lord Fauntleroy in modern dress has a rough time with his more informal contemporaries.

We have seen such an instance among our study children. One set of parents had precise and sharply defined standards of politeness and courteous behavior. Their careful thank-yous, bows, and shaking of hands did not appear inappropriate for them as adults. They had trained their youngster to be just as formal. For him, as a four-year-old in a middle-class New York suburban area, this style of behavior looked pretentious, stuffy, and even pedantic. When he went to nursery school, he became an object of ridicule and the butt of other children's jokes, which bewildered and confused him. The remedy lay in unlearning what he had learned about manners. He had to start all over again to adopt behavior appropriate to his age and social group.

In this case the issue was not between good and bad manners. It was between *functional* manners which serve to make relationships with others easier and *formalistic* manners which have the opposite effect.

In most circles, for example, a pleasant "Hi" and a wave is a more acceptable greeting from a small child to his next-door adult neighbor, and therefore better functional manners, than it would be for him to go over and carefully extend his right hand to the neighbor as she is shaking her mop over the porch.

In some social circles people don't observe the formality of having children help grownups with their chairs at the table. They wouldn't expect children under sixteen to hold coats for their guests when they're leaving. It's a good idea for parents to give some thought to the kind of manners they want children to observe before they begin to teach them.

Lessons should be suited not only to a child's age but to his ability to take them in and follow them. Almost any child picks up simply family rules for politeness long before he really understands what they're about. Saying "Thank you" when someone does something for him and "Please" when he wants something then gets to be automatic. He does it just the way a baby opens his mouth when he sees food coming. When he is a little older and begins to eat with the family, he learns to wait to eat until everyone is served, if his family expects it.

Manners outside the family are not always so easy for all children. You can see this at the end of a three-year-old's birthday party. One child rushes out, with his mother, hanging his head in embarrassment. Another curtseys and shakes hands with anyone she can find, saying, "The party was lovely. I hope you'll ask me again," or something equally spectacular. Another hugs the little hostess. Another holds out a limp hand and says a painful thank-you, and still another runs out, leaving his mother to say his thank-you for him.

The mother of the child who is too shy to say, "Thank you," will hold his hand and say, "Peter had a nice time at your party, Sally. Thank you." Gradually Peter will learn to get out a whispered thank-you of his own, and by the time he's five or six, he may even be able to look his hostess in the eye when he says good-bye.

The noisy, active, distractible child who bounds out of the party like a mouse from a trap the moment the door is opened will need lots of reminding, plus a restraining hand, before he remembers how to behave when a party's over. It will also take time for him to remember the rules for eating with grownups. The parents could start by letting him come to the table for dessert only. But no matter how gradually they start or how much the routine is modified to suit the child's capacities, the rules should be clearly established and maintained consistently.

"It may seem silly to struggle over getting a three-year-old to say, "Thank you," but the lesson establishes the concept of consideration for others, which is the basis for good manners. The harder it is for a child to get this message, the more important it may be to start instilling it early.

Efforts are not always successful. In fact, they may frequently produce rather firm resistance. The important thing is not to take the resistance personally or read into it a symptom of emotional distress. The approach should be just as matter-of-fact and helpful as with any lesson in discipline.

If learning is not progressing, the parent should first re-evaluate the issue. A child who appears to be resisting learning to say, "Thank you," may still be shy with adults and require time until he can begin to speak up easily with them. On the other hand, if this is not a problem, the parent can persist quietly and patiently in helping the child to learn.

Sometimes, paradoxically, children's manners deteriorate as a result of an advance in development. The youngster who now wants to feed himself may yank the spoon away from his mother and snap, "Don't touch my meat." At a later age, when he begins to want privacy, a child may order the parent to "Get out of my room" and to "Get out of the bathroom." He tends to be overassertive, at first, about each advance toward independence. This crudeness usually passes by itself. When it doesn't after a reasonable time, a few reminders about family standards of politeness usually serve to restore good manners.

If parents are consistent and patient and treat their children with the same understanding and consideration they expect, enforcement of reasonable demands will not create parent-child battles. Nor will it produce children so docile that anyone can push them around.

Children first learn to think of other people by being taught how to behave in clear-cut situations. Next they realize that their parents are considerate, too. At the same time, they can discover that there are times when it is important to consider one's needs first. Then they will know how to say no—politely.

12 SEX AND MODESTY

Fifty years ago sex was such an embarrassing subject that a good middle-class parent had trouble saying the word out loud. Only chickens had breasts. Adolescent girls grew chests or busts—in more advanced circles, bosoms.

Things have changed. The facts of life are spread before the small child like major-league batting averages. Nakedness is no longer taboo. Parents are often quite comfortable dressing while they help the children with their homework. In fact, they are generally so convinced of the importance of being open, free, and uninhibited that they sometimes feel guilt about demanding any privacy at all.

When Sigmund Freud published his paper on infantile sexuality early in the century, the idea that infants and young children might be aware of their sexual organs and even get pleasure from stimulating them was shocking even to the medical profession. Nevertheless, Freud's theory that neurosis originates from repression of the instinctual sexual drive in childhood has had profound influence on prevailing attitudes toward sex. Even many of those who find the theory open to question accept the corollary assumption that parents' feelings and teaching about sex affect children's sexual adjustment in adult life. This point of view is in large part responsible for the frank and open approach to sex in most enlightened families today.

The transformation is all to the good. However, the campaign to banish prudery has created some confusion. Parents may not be upset when children masturbate, as *their* parents were, but they are sometimes afraid to tell children when not to masturbate. They may feel awkward about teaching a three-year-old to put his pants on before he leaves the bathroom. They may feel strangely guilty about asking their children to stay out of their bedrooms unless invited. They don't dare admit that they would rather bathe or use the toilet in private.

When Jimmy asks in the bus, "Why has that lady got such a big stomach?" they feel compelled to tell the entire story of reproduction right then and there, even though they feel the place is inappropriate. When Sally asks for a rundown on the differences between men and women, they're afraid to suggest that the explanation they are offering is not for general neighborhood consumption.

Basically, there is often a tendency to confuse personal modesty, the desire for privacy, and reasonable consideration for social convention, with prudery. Perhaps sex education should be redefined. It originated as part of the campaign to make sex respectable. Parents, brought up by Victorians, wanted their own children to have healthy, unself-conscious feelings about sex. They knew that the extreme prudish taboos of a respectable, middle-class family of 1900 were bad influences on the children. They were also concerned that their own anxieties, inhibitions, and problems regarding sex should not be transmitted to their children. The popularization of Freud's theories also increased the conviction of the importance of early uninhibited knowledge of sex. Freud asserted that infants had definite sexual feelings, that these sex urges evolved into adult sexuality, and that interference with the predetermined sequence of sexual evolution was a basic cause for neurosis. Therefore, if a child had a bad start with sex—so these theories would have it—his adult sex life and even his whole personality could be warped.

To avoid any implication that childish curiosity was wrong or shameful, parents began presenting the mechanics of sex as fully and calmly as possible. The facts of life were administered on demand. Children were not embarrassed by parental interference with any investigation of their bodies. Masturbation, like thumbsucking, was anticipated and not discouraged. Children's unconcern about their own and others' naked bodies was guarded by studied noninterference. This approach was expected to keep children from feeling guilty about their bodies, their feelings, and their natural curiosity. The object was to prevent repression of sexual thoughts and urges that would then find outlet in neurotic ways. Sexual development, instead, would proceed in normal, uninhibited fashion and help insure happy marriage.

The revolution in sexual attitudes, however, has not produced any dramatic decline in neurosis or in the divorce rate. Unhealthy parental handling of sex may *help* create emotional problems for children. But this is certainly not the major cause of neurosis. Nor does sexual know-how and an uninhibited upbringing provide a hard and fast guarantee of marital success. The many qualities of mind and heart that make possible a satisfying and enduring marriage develop out of all the experiences and influences from infancy, through childhood and adolescence, to maturity.

An adult sexual relationship is the most intimate of all social relationships. As such it reflects not only the individual's attitudes about sex, but also his feelings of self-worth and self-respect, as well as his attitudes toward other people. This concept of the social nature of sex was pioneered by the culturalist group of psychoanalysts, led by Karen Horney, Harry Stack Sullivan, Clara Thompson, and Erich Fromm, who rejected Freud's biological approach to sex. It has come to be accepted even by most of the strictly Freudian psychoanalysts.

The simpler part of sex education is telling children what they want to know about their bodies and about how babies are born. There are a number of helpful guidebooks. The principal advice is to answer questions simply and directly when they arise. Inexperienced parents, eager to satisfy their children's curiosity, often make the mistake of plunging into a subject much more deeply than is either necessary or useful. This failing is so common that it has become the subject of a whole series of jokes. The best known, perhaps, is about the mother whose seven-year-old son runs into the house asking, "Where did I come from, Mommy?" The mother launches into the details of procreation, finally getting back, a little reluctantly, to the primal scene. When she finishes, the little boy looks at her as quizzically as at the beginning and says, "But I want to know where I *come* from. Johnny says he was born in Texas, but you've never told me where I was born."

The degree of curiosity children exhibit about sex varies. Some ask questions and come back to the subject frequently as they grow older. Others ask very few questions and seem to have little interest in their bodies, how babies are born, why people get married, etc.

The outward expression of interest in sex often corresponds with the amount of curiosity and inquisitiveness a child shows in general. A child who peppers his parents with "whys" about everything he sees—"What makes it rain?" "How does an auto work?" "Why does fire smoke?" "Why are some buildings tall and some short?"—is usually full of questions about sex. The less openly curious child is not as inquisitive, as a rule, about his body or where babies come from. However, when a very curious child asks nothing about sex, or a noncurious one becomes almost compulsively inquisitive in this one area, parents should look for the reasons. If they question tactfully, they may discover that the child has misinterpreted a snatch of adult conversation or been frightened and confused by something he has seen or by another child's wild story. A matter-of-fact discussion may be very useful in clearing up the child's confusion and anxiety.

Often it is hard to know what a three-year-old wants to know when he asks, "Where did I come from?" The simplest answer is usually the best. "From my belly." One can be sure that if this answer is not satisfactory, a child will ask again. It is also generally true that the information given the first time will not suffice forever. Six months or a year later the child will probably ask again. This time he may want more or different information. It will again serve for a while; then he will ask again. And no matter how skillfully he is answered, or how often, chances are that his picture of sex and reproduction at age eleven or twelve will still be incomplete. But what he *will* have that his grandmother certainly did not is an easy feeling about this whole area of life. He will not be afraid to find out more nor will he be ashamed of his curiosity.

The way parents answer questions is also important. The child should be taken seriously and not talked down to. It is often a temptation for parents to quote their children's naïve but earnest questions about sex for the amusement of dinner guests, but it is a temptation that should be avoided. Children overhear more often than is generally suspected, and nothing shuts off their confidences as effectively as realizing that they are being made fun of.

Part of a child's unself-consciousness will come from the natural way his parents have talked to him and part from their casual attitude towards their children's bodies and their own. Such a casual attitude is possible when parents recognize that parts of the body that have sexual connotation for them have not yet developed such special meaning to the young child. Children used to be brought up not to touch or even look at certain parts of their bodies. Now their parents bathe, pat, and admire them—in whole and in part, naked as well as clothed.

There remain, however, some confusions, left over from the early days of reaction against Victorian prudery. Parents used to punish children who masturbated or frighten them with tales of what might happen if they continued. The newly enlightened generation, assured that the practice is not abnormal, is sometimes so afraid of what might happen if they interfered that they don't tell their children: "People don't do that in public." It is important to remember that teaching children to be aware of the impression they make and the effect they have on others, to be responsive to social demands, and to develop a feeling of personal modesty are as much a part of healthy sexual adjustment as growing up uninhibited.

All the evidence indicates that the infant's discovery of his genitals is quite accidental. It happens just the way he finds his fingers, toes, mouth, ears, hair, or his mother's locket when she bends over him. Feeling his genitals becomes masturbation, later, if he repeatedly and habitually stimulates this area.

It is no more dangerous to interfere with a baby's holding his penis in order to be able to change his diaper more quickly than it would be to take his thumb out of his mouth to wash his face. This is a matter of convenience and doesn't negate the reasonable and widely accepted permissive attitude towards the baby's handling of his genitals. Permissiveness in private, however, is not the same as permissiveness in public. It is a mistake for a mother not to make clear to a child, as soon as he is old enough to respond to any social demand (age three or four), that people don't masturbate in public. If parents do not make this clear, they risk exposing the child to public scolding, ridicule, and even ostracism. Thus, failing to teach the difference between what's appropriate in private and what is acceptable in public could lead to the very confusion and anxiety modern sex education hopes to avoid.

If a child continues to masturbate in public after his fifth birthday, one would suspect that something is troubling him. However, it is first necessary to make sure that the youngster really knows better. Sometimes, for fear of making a child feel guilty, parents really don't tell him clearly to stop. They divert and distract rather than simply say, "Stop." However, if a child continues masturbating openly when the practice has been plainly forbidden, a psychiatrist should be consulted. The problem may be that of a negative, teasing youngster using the trick he knows will annoy his exhausted parents. Or it may be that for any number of reasons a child has not made the normal discovery of more engrossing attractions in the world around him. This is usually indicative of more serious psychological disturbance. At this age it is equally a matter of concern if a child retreats frequently to private masturbation and seems less than normally involved with toys, playmates, and the activity of people around him.

There are other situations where parents fail to indicate that modesty is appropriate. They start out dressing and undressing before their babies, going to the bathroom with them, bathing with them. Later, they are uncomfortable about teaching the usual conventions and making their children aware of everyone's wish for privacy. They don't know how to tell the toddler to put his pants on in the bathroom, how to stop Jimmy's questions about the pregnant lady on the bus. They're awkward about closing doors or telling children not to enter without knocking.

But it is no harder for a child to recognize the limitations that society and personal preference put on his behavior than it is to learn other social customs and forms of politeness. "You don't come into the living room without your pants because people keep their clothes on in public."

"You don't talk about the lady over there. It's bad manners. We'll talk about it when we get home."

"You must knock before you come into my room because sometimes people like to be alone."

Directions should be as simple as that.

If parents don't teach the distinction between what's appropriate at home and what's acceptable in public, the child may learn it painfully outside from less broad-minded adults who equate his naïve unself-consciousness with a kind of moral degeneracy.

The facts of life are important for a child's healthy psychological development. So is a relaxed attitude about sex and a feeling that sexual curiosity is normal. It is just as important to know when modesty is appropriate and when the privacy of others should be respected. These qualities are among the many that contribute to the capacity for mature love. By themselves, they do not guarantee it. Many other influences in the family and in society at large contribute throughout the childhood years. Perhaps the most important part of sex education is education unrelated to sex and reproduction as such, but concerned with the development of decent social values, self-respect, and respect for others. Without this over-all healthy social development, free and uninhibited sex can easily be used primarily in the service of unhealthy goals: proof of power, exploitation of others, self-aggrandizement, and so on. A combination of good social and personal values, together with healthy attitudes and accurate information about sex, can give children a good start towards sexual maturity.

13 NEW SITUATIONS

For the grownup most of life is routine, but for the infant almost all experience is new, and he has to cope constantly with the unfamiliar. A newborn baby is hardly accustomed to the hospital nursery, when he has to go home. He has just gotten acquainted with his family when he is plunked into a bath. He gets fond of his formula, finally, when he has to deal with Pablum and bananas, vitamin drops and meat, and an enormous number of strange tastes, textures, temperatures, and smells.

The way in which a child responds to new situations is important. It may determine how quickly or slowly he adjusts to a new person, place, or thing. It may influence his attitude when he anticipates a new experience. It may make a big difference in the way other people react to him.

The child who can meet the new and unfamiliar easily and cheerfully has a decided advantage. The toddler who bounces into a roomful of new people bursting with curiosity and zest gets a smiling welcome. This adventurous, outgoing type meets with few brush-offs. As a result, he usually views the world as a delightful place full of friendly, helpful people. Successive good experiences fortify this attitude. He makes friends sooner. Life with him is easy for his parents, and this inevitably makes life pleasant for him.

At the other extreme is the child who has a tantrum when he has to deal with the strange and new. He can't seem to adjust quickly to a change of scene. He usually shies away from a new face. He is distressed at the prospect of trying anything different, from skates to arithmetic. Grownups and children, too, have a hard time getting interested in a youngster who stays on the side lines, answers questions in monosyllables, and rejects their first efforts to make him happy.

In our study we have been able to gather information on the different ways in which children react to the new. The differences have been evident in the first months of life. Most of the children have retained their characteristic pattern as they have grown older.

The child's reaction to the new is made up of several temperamental characteristics acting together. The basic consideration is whether he tends to have a positive response (approach) or a negative one (withdrawal) to the unfamiliar. With either approach or withdrawal his reaction may be mild or intense and show low or high activity. If his first response is negative, he may change to a positive one rapidly (quick adaptability) or gradually (slow adaptability).

A number of different combinations are possible. For example, in responding to the first taste of applesauce at three months, one infant swallows, smiles, waves his hands, and reaches forward with mouth open for the next mouthful, while another infant also swallows, opens his mouth for each new mouthful, but sits quietly with little or no facial expression. Still another spits out the first mouthful, clamps his mouth tight, and twists his whole body away. If the parent persists he cries loudly. He continues to object with diminishing intensity for a week, then begins to swallow the applesauce. Several weeks later he is eating the food with great gusto.

Two other infants do not swallow, sit quietly, and let the food dribble out of their mouths. With each new mouthful they repeat this performance with no fussing but only a slight turning aside of the head. The mothers of both infants offer the applesauce each day. One baby begins to take it in three days, the other only after three weeks.

The differences in children can be seen when they are brought at age three to a new playground. One toddler runs at once to a group of strange boys and girls and within a few minutes is laughing and jumping with them. A second youngster howls and kicks until his mother takes him home. The second day he also cries, but less, and by the fifth day he is ready to join the group. A week later he is a lusty, ebullient leading citizen of the playground. Another walks in slowly and quietly the first trip, but joins the group quickly. Another child holds back, pulls away when his mother tries to urge him, but after standing on the side lines watching for an hour, moves in slowly. Another youngster also holds back, but does not move toward the group at all the first day. The next day he edges in a little. Each successive day he moves a little closer to the group until he becomes a quiet but active member after the first week.

Many children adapt quickly and easily to new situations. The more vigorous and intense seem to plunge in as if they had been told what to expect and had figured out what to do in advance. The less active and milder ones move in easily but quietly. Both types tend to approach other people with an air of assurance and friendliness that gives them an easy entree to individuals and groups.

Many other children have a little initial hesitation with something unfamiliar. But they adapt very quickly, and the first holding back may be so brief and inconspicuous as to be hardly noticeable. They rarely have real problems with the new. Parents and teachers wait almost without thinking, offering help so unobtrusively that they are often hardly aware of what they are doing.

If such a child is going into a new place, his mother or father holds his hand until *he* lets go. If he's joining a new group of people, a mother might point out a child he has known before or a familiar toy. Offering new foods to a baby, she may take a taste herself, saying, "Mmm! Some for Timmy?" with a smile. In most cases the child's positive response is so quick that parents, looking back, forget any initial hesitation he may have had. If you ask them what Sue or Sammy did in a new situation, they'll report, "Oh, she just moved in," or "Sammy likes everything right off."

Some children are slower and more hesitant at first meetings. They are shy but *not* anxious. Such children may *become* anxious if parents or other people make them believe there is something wrong with them for being shy.

A minority of youngsters have prolonged initial negative reactions. Some are intense and active; others are mild and quiet.

Those children who protest the new violently may lose no time in declaring themselves soon after birth. They cry, hold their breath, turn red in their first bath, and repeat the performance for many baths to come. They may go through the same routine with their first solid food, or when they are put in a playpen or high chair for the first time, or left with grandmother for the afternoon.

Instead of cooing back at those who coo into their carriages, they may try to bury themselves in their pillows, screaming lustily until the strange face disappears and the reassuring arms of a familiar friend are tightly around them.

These violent protests may make it seem as if they never adapt. Nevertheless, they finally come to like their baths. They eventually put away just as much Pablum as the next fellow. In time they even stop screaming at every new face and learn to make friends. If not rushed or pressured at the beginning, they gradually cope with the new experiences that come along naturally in a child's life. When they do adapt, their vigor and intensity often become assets. From being outsiders at first, they may eventually turn into leaders.

The children who withdraw quietly are not as dramatic in their protests, but can usually be spotted quickly. They lie still in the bath, maybe frowning or whimpering. They let new foods dribble out of their mouths. They turn their heads away when a strange face comes too close. They fuss and whine, but rarely bellow.

These youngsters also finally adapt if given enough time, and they become quiet but contented participators.

Parents may be disappointed when an infant doesn't warm up quickly to strange people or to unfamiliar surroundings, but they usually do not make a big problem out of it. They accept the fact that it takes their baby longer than other infants to adjust to anything new. They give him more time to get used to new things, more chances to try new experiences, and as much help as they can in making him feel at home in new situations.

However, when the same baby becomes a toddler who clings to his mother in the playground or has a tantrum at the entrance to the birdhouse at the zoo, it is another story. Some mothers and fathers forget that the youngster has always warmed up slowly to new ways, sights, and sounds, or people and places. Instead of letting him proceed in his own way at his own pace, they now read his hesitation and clinging as excessive shyness or insecurity or sheer obstinacy. They mistake his slow way of learning new things for dullness. They start to worry about the future: How will he get along in the world? Will he make friends? Who would like him? Will he ever be able to get into college? They get panicky or guilty or angry, and begin to put pressure on the child.

It is not only parents who mistake this temperamental characteristic of initial withdrawal and slow adaptability for pathological behavior. Some teachers, psychologists, and psychiatrists react the same way. If the child clings to his mother in a strange playground, he must have "separation anxiety." If he screams and kicks when brought suddenly into an unfamiliar group, he must be "hostile" and "aggressive." A child who behaves this way may have a true behavior problem. On the other hand, he may be showing his individual temperamental response to a new situation.

It is sensible, however, for parents to be concerned when a child's reactions to the new are persistently negative. The way a child reacts when he joins a new group or starts a new subject in school can affect the whole course of that particular experience. If a five-year-old who adapts slowly looks blank and hangs his head when a new teacher asks his name, the teacher is apt to get the impression that he's slow and treat him accordingly. He may be just as smart as the child next to him who finally answers for him, but it won't look that way. The ten-year-old who goes to camp for the first time may take so long to sort out her bunkmates that all alliances will be formed by the time she's ready to choose a friend.

The "slow warmer-up" does need a helping hand. However, well-intentioned measures are often anything but helpful. Pushing such a child against his nature can make him slower. Forcing him to move before he is ready, abandoning him where he can't cope, or imposing impossible demands, all make him retreat rather than move forward. Too much pressure, in fact, may turn a child who adapts slowly into just the kind of child his parents dread—excessively shy, afraid to try anything new, and therefore seriously handicapped in learning and making friends. If wisely handled, however, he becomes sociable, makes friends, and may wind up doing as well as or better than many faster, more sparkling performers.

Vignettes from the life of Joey illustrate how a child's fundamental difficulty in adapting may diminish with age and experience —*if that experience is fruitful.*

Fortunately for Joey, his parents were understanding and patient. He was against everything from the start. When he was three and a half his family took a two-week camping vacation in Maine. It seemed like a huge mistake for the first week. Joey sat on a blanket in front of the tent and screamed whenever a bug came near. His parents tried to take him to the water. He howled when his feet touched the pebbles. They wanted him to feel the grass and pick flowers. He reacted as if he had been laid on a bed of needles. Then, suddenly, on the eighth day of the vacation, Joey got up and followed his father into the water. A few minutes later his father was cold and wanted to get out and get dressed. He had a hard time persuading Joey that they'd had enough. Joey never went back to his blanket after that. Six days later, when it was time to go home, he was ready to settle in Maine.

That fall he went to nursery school. His mother showed him his locker. He refused to hang his jacket in it. He saw the classroom, but he would not go in. His mother stood at the door with him and looked in. After an hour they went home. The next day he followed her into the classroom still wearing his jacket. He sat down beside his mother on the window seat all morning. When she got up to look at a toy, hoping to interest him, he followed and watched. He never tried to take the toy from her, and when she sat down again, he sat down, too.

On the third morning he sat for a few minutes, then got up quietly and began to play with a truck. The teacher suggested that his mother leave, but she postponed that step until the following day. She knew that if she pushed, Joey would have to begin all over. On the next day he did *not* sit beside her when school started, but went straight to his truck. She took that cue, said, "I'll be back," and left with a breezy wave.

Joey stayed in school. At first he brushed off other children's efforts to join his play and didn't join theirs. In January his teacher said she thought he was insecure and withdrawn. His mother said, "Don't rush him." By the end of the year Joey's games in the sandbox with trucks, pulleys, and five helpers were one of the favorite activities of the whole group. Joey had found *his* way. By the end of the first year in nursery school a casual observer, looking in on the three-year-olds, could not have picked out the child who, in September, looked as if he would *never* settle into nursery school.

That was eleven years ago. This fall Joey started high school. He turned down the opportunity to go to a new experimental school a little distance from home. His parents are sure his actual choice was determined by where most of his friends were going, rather than by the kind of courses or extracurricular activity the school offered. They are probably right. Joey will usually tend to avoid a completely new experience if he can. However, he has learned a great deal about moving into places where he feels strange. He takes his time making friends, but he *acts* friendly. He knows that new problems will be hard for him the first time, so he manages to get extra help or extra practice with new work. When he was little, he would say "No" to any invitation that might expose him to the unfamiliar. If the family went hiking or to the beach, he would try to stay home. When he was five he'd cry. When he was seven he'd say he had homework or a book he wanted to finish, or a model to make. By the time he was nine he'd go when coaxed. Finally, when he went to high school for the first time, he told his father, "I don't know whether I'll like it, but I'll try. Right now I'm a little scared, but I guess it will work out O.K. It always has."

This is the moment that parents of children like Joey hope for. It came about because he had every help that parents could give.

First, his father and mother recognized that the toddler who didn't like parties, new clothes, and trips, and the baby who started life resisting his bath, new food, and strange beds, were the same child: negative, slow to adapt, and persistent. They didn't mistake these qualities for meanness, sullenness, obstinacy, stupidity, or excessive fear.

Second, they didn't try to change him into someone else. They didn't shove and push and harangue him to do things faster, speak up more, be more friendly. They didn't compare him unfavorably with the other children in the family. Instead, they were generally patient. They waited for his tantrums to stop, realizing that a tantrum occurred when the strain of some new encounter was too much for him. Rather than get angry, they comforted him. At the same time they did not consider his vulnerability an excuse for shielding him from life. They tried to give him as many opportunities as possible to learn that things weren't as bad as they seemed to him at first, and *might* even be enjoyable.

Third, they tried to make his experiences with the new and different as successful as possible. This was especially important. Even if the slow warmer-up remains negative and resistant to new situations as he grows up, no great harm is done if they work out well for him. Parents and grownups, like Joey's parents, can help a great deal. What can they do specifically to help such a child have successful new experiences?

Children who balk at new foods or places and hesitate to meet new people learn to adapt faster when the learning isn't interrupted. Such a little boy would have a hard time getting used to nursery school if he had frequent sore throats. Each time he stayed home he would have to start adjusting all over again. In fact, one would almost forgive the mother of a nonadaptive child if she occasionally sent him off to nursery school with mild sniffles during his first year there. Parents, however, cannot expect to prevent all interruptions in learning to adapt. But they can plan many events so as to avoid such interruptions. They can postpone a family trip until the youngster is safely adjusted to his new school or neighborhood. If they go to a new place for the summer, they can avoid any side trips to other new places for the first month.

A mother would certainly avoid shielding a diffident child from experiences that are hard for him. At the same time, she would try to do anything she could think of to make his encounters easier. No mother would expect a hesitant three-year-old to ask a storekeeper for a candy bar. She might ask the man for a candy bar for Tommy, for example. Next time she might ask Tommy what kind of candy bar he would like, hoping he would tell the storekeeper. Later she might say, "You tell Mr. X what you want." If he didn't seem up to that she might give him the money for the candy, saying, "You pay Mr. X for the candy." Tommy would probably do that proudly. Perhaps the next time, or the one after that, he would ask for candy himself, in response to his mother's suggestions.

A mother would not take such a child to a birthday party full of strange children. She might try to have him meet a friend who also was going and have them go together. Or she might stay with him at the party until he found a friend or a favorite toy or something he was interested in doing. She might invent a job for him (with the hostess' help), such as cleaning up the wrappings from the presents or putting napkins on the table.

Some children always react to new tasks with "I can't *ever* do that." It helps for the grownup to remind them of past triumphs. The child who says he can never do multiplication, after the first lesson, may begin to try if he's reminded that he said the same thing about reading, even though he now reads well and enjoys it.

Parents sometimes make the mistake of interpreting hesitancy and deliberation as fear. They expect the three-year-old to react as they do. If their toddler doesn't rush into a new group the way they breeze into a cocktail party, they immediately assume that he's scared. He may or may not be scared, but he has to take his time. It doesn't help him when his mother rushes in to "help." She may try to get him to play with someone he doesn't want to play with at all or someone who doesn't want to play with him. She may try to get him started at something he doesn't want to do, just at the moment when he has decided what he does want to do. She upsets *his* own equilibrium, interferes with his learning how to adapt, and often puts him in a spot where he can't help failing.

There is a vast difference between a deliberate child and a frightened one, as the reactions of three four-year-olds, left to play at a friend's house for the first time, will show.

The first one stands still with his friends and looks around. The friend says, "Want to play with my toys?"

The guest keeps on standing still and silent. He is really "casing the joint," deciding how to enjoy himself. In a few minutes he goes over to the blocks, gets some cars, and says, "I'll build a garage. Then we can ride the cars all around."

The second child's response to his friend's invitation is a little different. He says nothing, but finally he begins to build a garage and play, almost silently, except when the friend takes something he wants to use. However, when his mother comes for him, he suddenly comes to life, pushes her away, and begs her to let him play some more.

The third child, instead of beginning to play, succumbs to fear. The tears roll down his face, and he sobs, "I want my mommy."

When a child's approach to new experience is slow and deliberate, he learns to adjust more easily and quickly if he is given some encouragement and allowed to take his time. Too much pushing or interference disrupts his own style of adjusting and keeps him from gaining the ability to move more smoothly to the strange and unfamiliar as he grows up.

14 THE DIFFICULT CHILD

Early in Mrs. B.'s first pregnancy, she was asked to take care of a friend's five-week-old baby girl for an afternoon. Mrs. B. was a little hesitant, but her friend was reassuring. "She'll let you know what she wants. If she cries, change her diaper. If she still cries, feed her. She may drink four ounces. But burp her after two. When she pushes the nipple out of her mouth, she's had enough."

It sounded easy, and it was. Everything happened exactly as predicted. The friend came home to find both baby and substitute mother doing well. And Mrs. B. was convinced that she had exceptional natural talents for motherhood.

Some months later she changed her mind. Her own baby, Linda, was born. Mrs. B. was first baffled and then alarmed to discover, after coming home from the hospital, that there was apparently no way she could make her *own* daughter comfortable.

Linda would cry frequently day and night—sometimes for a few minutes, sometimes for an hour or more. Usually, no definite reason for the crying could be found. Linda might take some milk or she might refuse it. She might burp or she might not. Walking with her, patting her back, rocking her—nothing seemed to help.

This went on for days. Finally, in real despair, Mrs. B. called her friend and tearfully confessed her failure. "I'm a terrible mother. Can you help me?" Fortunately, her friend's older child had also been a difficult infant to take care of. The friend was able to reassure Mrs. B. that Linda was undoubtedly a normal baby even if she was not "easy." Her behavior had nothing to do with whether her own mother was good or bad, or her mother's friend better or worse. Rather, it reflected the child's individual temperament. She was a difficult baby. When baby nurses and pediatricians talk about "easy" babies and "difficult" ones, they know whereof they speak. They have watched hundreds of new babies take their first food, their first naps, and their first baths. They have seen the differences in the way infants react to dressing and undressing, to feeding, and to cuddling. And the differences in the babies' behavior are plain to see. The common notion that the parent is always responsible when babies are restless, fussy, and unpredictable is not supported by the evidence. The parents of the difficult babies in our study were not better or worse than the parents of easy ones. These findings only confirm what many experienced pediatricians and nurses have long known.

Fortunately for inexperienced mothers, most babies are "easy." Very soon after birth they settle down to a regular schedule of eating and sleeping. They make at most only a brief fuss about changes in the routines of their daily lives. On balance, their behavior is predominantly pleasant and sunny. But a small minority —in our experience from seven to ten babies in every hundred— are not easy at all.

Their habits are irregular. The don't establish definite hunger and sleeping patterns that are predictable from day to day. They don't have bowel movements regularly. They tend to have negative withdrawal reactions to most new stimuli and situations. In addition, they are not easily adaptable, and almost every change in their routines involves a struggle.

Their moods are predominantly negative. Unlike the average five-week-old baby who begins to smile and wriggle when a stranger playfully dangles a rattle above him, the negative child may turn away and start howling. The reactions of such youngsters are also frequently intense. When they cry, they often bellow; and their laugh, too, is loud and long.

We don't know what makes these babies the way they are. Only future research can determine what physiological factors are responsible for the specific temperamental facts of irregularity, slow adaptability, withdrawal reactions, and predominantly negative mood. But we do know what does *not* account for their temperaments.

In the first place, we have found no evidence of pathology in these babies. There were no more complications in pregnancy and delivery, no more signs of brain injury or congenital disease, than among easy babies. Adaptive development, both physical and mental, progressed as normally. The babies are neither smarter nor less intelligent, better or less well coordinated, healthier or more sickly than easy babies.

Nor can we find any evidence that mothers of difficult babies are responsible for their style of behavior. As a group, they are not different from other mothers. Some are efficient and some are inept; some cuddle and play with their children, and others are less demonstrative and more businesslike; some keep the babies spick and span, others are casual about their appearance; some bundle the babies up, others leave them free. The personal relations between mothers and fathers in this group also spread over a very wide range.

The difficult baby is not easy to feed, to put to sleep, to bathe, or to dress. His parents cannot count on sleeping through the night without his awakening once or more, crying. When he is ill his care becomes even more burdensome.

These babies may be called "vulnerable," because they have more difficulty in coping with change and stress. As a result, they have tended to develop more behavior problems than the other children in our study group.

The more irregular and nonadaptive they are, the more they need firm, steady, patient, and consistent care. But it is not always easy for even the best of parents to be patient and consistent with a difficult child. When the child keeps screaming for something he wants, it is always tempting for the parent either to yield in order to re-establish peace and quiet, or to enter into battle and insist that the crying stop at once. Both temptations are increased when the problem comes up daily and in many different forms.

If, in addition, the parents assume that their baby is difficult because they don't love him enough, they are almost certainly going to make him *more* difficult. The baby's irregular functioning and frequent crying make them think the child is maladjusted. They automatically blame themselves, assuming that the child is unhappy because he has been frustrated too much, not loved enough, or unconsciously rejected. This guilt then keeps them from following through consistently on the kind of training program the child needs.

For example, a mother may decide, when her baby is six months old, that she must finally put him on some kind of regular schedule, whether he eats or not, or screams or not. She tries this for a day or two, but the screaming claws at her conscience. She wonders whether she is making matters worse, perhaps building up hostility that will never mend. She abandons her efforts to establish a routine in favor of more and more love and attention.

But more love, affection, and immediate response to the baby's demands doesn't change the picture. Love, apparently, is not enough. The infant continues to wake up at all hours of the night, to eat in a completely unpredictable fashion, and to cry loud and long. Eventually, one or both parents give up or blow up. Then follows another brief period of stern discipline, often drastically administered. This only serves to increase the baby's resistances and negative reactions. Open resentment toward the baby may now develop, only to be followed by a new wave of guilt and remorse. Confusion over what is happening then easily leads to disagreements between husband and wife over what to do next, perhaps with each using different tactics with the baby.

The parents of the difficult babies in our study have run the gamut of these possible reactions: patient acceptance, helplessness, guilt, and resentment with punitive tendencies. In any parent pair, one response usually predominated, though many showed mixed feelings.

Roger's father was pleased to have such a "lusty" youngster. He cheerfully told us how loud and long Roger howled with his first baths, new foods, strangers, and vaccinations. But the father knew Roger would always settle down eventually "and then he's such a pleasure." The mother was not so sure this lustiness was a virtue. She was periodically uneasy and guilty, felt she must be a bad mother, and even became mildly depressed over Roger's recurrent crying and difficulties with sleeping and feeding.

But her husband not only reassured her; he pitched in with the care of this difficult child. This helped the mother maintain a patient, consistent, and positive approach. The parents were rewarded as Roger became a toddler and then a schoolboy.

His adjustment to routines became increasingly smooth, his behavior showed fewer negative reactions, and he did indeed become a lusty, exuberant youngster.

Barbara's parents, by contrast, were dismayed and helpless at having such a loud, negative, and nonadaptive child. They already had an older child with a serious medical problem. Their own earlier lives had been filled with difficult struggles. They yearned for peace and quiet, but could not find it with Barbara. When things went her own way, Barbara was a delightful little girl. But when the parents had to stick to routines and schedules, there frequently were commotions and tantrums lasting up to several hours. The parents gave in each time. The father was frank about it. "I know I should let her cry it out, but I can't stand the noise. It isn't worth it. I'd rather give in." The result was a household largely run by Barbara. Her preferences for mealtimes, bedtime, going out or not going out, came to be the major factor in fixing the household schedules.

David, too, was a youngster who was typically what his parents called an "againster." In infancy, this meant only that most new routines involved an uncomfortable week or so until the baby accepted them and stopped his crying, fussing reaction. As David grew older, the negative reactions became more formidable. Whenever the family set out on a trip, he objected when he was taken out, and when it was time to return home, he objected to its ending. In each case his protests were loud and long. By the time he was five and six, his parents approached most new situations with a sense of reluctance. Increasingly, they considered David a trial. By contrast, his brother, two years his junior, and his sister, two years younger than that, approached each change in scene and activity with positive, outgoing responses that made any time spent with them a delight.

The more David's parents became aware of how they felt about him and how differently they felt about his brother and sister, the guiltier they felt. They promised each other to be more positive toward David, but to no avail. They became more and more convinced that their negative attitude was the cause of his difficult behavior and could not be persuaded that the truth was exactly the opposite. The guiltier they felt, the more difficult it became for them to make demands on David or insist on his learning the rules of social living. The more this intimidation by guilt went on, the more David became an uncooperative, self-centered member of the family.

Ann was also a difficult child. Her parents had started by trying to understand her demands and pleasing her when she was an infant. They expected this approach to turn her into an easy, cooperative child. But when Ann continued to be difficult to manage, her parents became impatient and then antagonistic. By the time she was five years old, their response to her showed a stronger and stronger component of punitiveness. Her father ordered her to go to bed without fussing, to stop sucking her thumb, to do what she was told without whining; and her failure to comply was met with shouting, spanking, and deprivation. Her mother vacillated between comforting the child when she thought Ann was frightened and blowing up when her balking behavior interfered outrageously with the morning timetable. Ann's little sister, who was not a difficult child, was handled with greater consistency and without punitiveness.

With each of these children—Roger, Barbara, David, and Ann —the parents were reacting to the characteristics of the child. And each parent responded on the basis of his or her own personality. One parent saw primarily the good qualities of the child; another became guilty; and still another became punitive. The same parents were positive and relaxed with their easy children. They then appeared very much alike. The problems of managing their difficult children, on the other hand, highlighted their individual reactions to stress.

Resentment, guilt, and vacillation in the parent only lead to increasing negative responses in the difficult child, and set the stage for the development of a behavior problem. Fortunately, the situation normally does not deteriorate this badly. Most parents of difficult babies in our study were consistent and patient enough so that at most only mild problems developed.

The difficult baby does not have to turn into the rebellious, negative, dissatisfied, fretful child. Although he poses problems for the hardiest parent, these are not insurmountable. He is not an easily adaptable baby, but he can learn to like things. He is a very intense little human being, and his protests can raise the roof and sear the nerve ends, but his intensity can have positive uses.

During infancy, the rose may seem very well concealed among the thorns, but the vision is worth cherishing during the long discouraging early months when patient, tireless, good-humored consistency must be maintained to establish the simplest routines and schedules, and soften the edges of the difficult baby's nature.

It may seem that he will never give his parents a whole night's rest, but if the parents' patience in maintaining bedtime routines is as firm as his protests, he will finally learn to live by the law. Every instance in which he learns to adapt to a simple routine will be a milestone of progress toward greater general adaptability.

The first eighteen months are the hardest. During this period, the new baby is gradually introduced to the world around him. He learns the flavors of a full range of foods; meets many new people; adjusts to crib, playpen, carriage, stroller; learns to sit, stand, walk, run, feed himself, play with other children, visit doctors and shoe stores, barbers and restaurants.

If the difficult baby adapts to all these basic kinds of experience with a modicum of grace, the following years will be easy by comparison. The mission is accomplished little by little, one step at a time. There are several things to avoid. The child should not be loaded with too many demands or new adjustments at one time. For example, one would not have a new doctor give the baby shots on his first visit, and would not leave the child with a new sitter right after moving to a new apartment.

It is often helpful to have the father step in when the going gets too rough, when the mother is overtired or her nerves frayed. This may save the day, prevent a blowup by the mother, and avoid the setback that inevitably results from letting demands go by the board "just this once." The difficult baby who has almost accepted going to the barber, for example, will be just as difficult as ever the next time if his mother relents at the barbershop door and takes him home.

Once basic routines are accepted, parents can begin to see the sunny side of the child. It may still be tough to move him from one activity or place to another, but even these adjustments will become more automatic, and the activities themselves become fun for mother and child. The baby who screamed and kicked and threw himself on the sidewalk in rebellion then becomes the toddler who works up more enthusiasm than anyone else for the people he likes, who plays familiar games with greater zest than any of the other children. Now that he is used to the playground and his friends, he is the most ebullient, most imaginative, most enthusiastic member of the gang. When he likes to go on family outings, he is the child who sees, hears, and communicates the most.

The temptation to give in to the often heart-rending protests of the fretful, difficult, irregular baby is always present. But he is not as despairing as he sounds. And the virtue of maintaining standards and schedules is very clearly demonstrated by the experiences of certain of these children in the study whom we have seen in connection with behavior problems.

The parents complained that these children didn't mind, didn't eat, would not play with other children, would not go to bed at night, would not take baths. Invariably, however, there were islands of healthy functioning. One child, for example, who was very intractable in general, was perfectly obedient and self-controlled about staying out of the street, waiting to cross with the lights, not touching electric plugs or hot irons. How did this happen? The mother had been clear in her own mind and consistently firm with the child where safety was involved, notwithstanding his usual tantrums when he was crossed. Consequently, he had learned the rules.

Another child had trouble in almost every department except eating. We found that the mother really didn't believe the child would starve and didn't have time to fuss with him at meals or supply them at odd intervals. She served his meals and took them away when he didn't eat. By the time he was three, he ate everything the family did without any fuss at all.

It may not always seem so, but it is easier to train the difficult baby than it is to *retrain* him once he has become a negativistic child. But even the negativistic child can be retrained. The parents themselves can do a great deal, depending on the severity of the problem and on their ability to change their tactics. When the negative behavior is limited or when it covers many areas but is expressed with moderation, handling the child differently may make a vast difference. The parents should deal with only one or two problems at a time, set up clear-cut, simple rules, and insist that they be observed. Then, if they maintain the rules quietly, patiently, and in a friendly fashion, the child gradually eases into compliance.

Part of retraining involves spelling out for the child the consequences of disobedience and putting these into effect promptly and consistently. For example, if the child dawdles in the morning but wants to get to nursery school on time, the parents might point out that if he dawdles over dressing he will be late. Then they must conscientiously refrain from rushing him or helping him dress at the last minute to keep him from being late. Similar tactics can usually be worked out simply and clearly for most of the problem behavior areas.

If such simple measures of training do not begin to bring results after a reasonable trial period of a month or so, it is then wise to seek professional advice and guidance.

15 PLAYING IN CHARACTER

When Nicky, one of the boys in our study, was five years old, his mother called us one day with an urgent problem. Nicky's nursery-school teacher had told her that he was an abnormally isolated and fearful child. At story hour all the other children listened, but he continued working on his railroad in the block corner. Other children played together on the slide in the playground, but Nicky almost always rode a tricycle by himself. It wasn't that he didn't *like* the children. He was pleasant when they joined his play. But the teacher felt he couldn't muster the courage to join someone else. Besides, he had a hard time giving up one activity and beginning another. She felt this was because he was afraid to move freely from one thing to another like the other children.

Nicky's mother and father were very upset, especially since they had not even noticed that anything was wrong.

After we reviewed our records of Nicky's development, it was easy for us to reassure the parents. They hadn't recognized Nicky's fears because he didn't have any more than were normal for a five-year-old boy. His teacher had fallen into the much too common trap of assuming there was only one kind of normal child. Her mental image of the normal child was a lively, active, gregarious boy or girl more interested in being with people than in what he was doing.

Nicky didn't fit the stereotype, but it was the stereotype, not Nicky, that was wrong. There was no more reason to attribute his style of play to fearfulness than there would be to conclude that a boy who chose to play chess rather than basketball was afraid of getting hurt.

We went over our reports on Nicky and reminded ⸢
the day he got a Tinker Toy set when he was fo⸤
father had left him in the morning with it, thinkin⸤
for a half hour and forget the toy. When they cam⸤
work in the evening he had copied the building on the b⸤
—during a solid five-hour work period.

This quiet, persistent little boy had been interested in how thi⸤
work from the time he could sit up. His understanding of mechanisms was far ahead of his playmates'. He was perfectly happy
when they wanted to share his interests, but not excited about
theirs. Children always came to play at his house, but he almost
never went to theirs. This was understandable behavior, considering the child. He showed no abnormal fears and never had.

It is a mistake to assume that there is *one* good way to play and
that any other way is abnormal. A child's play, like a grownup's
work, expresses what he is, what he likes, what's on his mind. How
dull for the world if all children played alike, all played together,
and all liked the same things. In play, as in daydreams (which are
a kind of play), children master the world, figure out their relationships to each other and to their parents. Play gives youngsters the
opportunity to find out more and more about the world around
them. They test themselves out, discover what their interests are
and what they are capable of doing. In play they try on roles as
they try on grownups' clothes.

On skates, on trikes, they learn the feeling of physical power
and mastery. With puzzles and construction sets they experience
the exhilaration of achievement. They stretch themselves physically, mentally, and emotionally

Sometimes, through play, they unscramble the experiences they
can't understand or banish the terror of those that frighten. One
little girl who had been bitten by a dog played over the experience
with her best doll for days afterward. "There, there," she would
comfort. "Don't cry, sweetie. The doggy didn't mean to hurt you.
He was just a baby puppy. He was afraid and he didn't know any
better." Finally she lost her fear of dogs and gave up this game.

Children frequently play hospital. One may have had a tonsillec-
tomy and be mastering her anxious memories of the event. Others

play because the doctor and nurse roles are so glamorous or perhaps, these days, because it's "just like on TV."

Play has so much meaning for children that psychiatrists use it as a basic method of studying and treating a problem child. A child often reveals his problems best in play. The psychiatrist then helps by guiding him to play out the solutions.

Children behave differently in their play because they *are* different. Some are more gregarious than others. Some are noisier and more active; others are more imaginative or more interested in doing things; some are more bossy, and so on.

The gregarious three-year-old goes into his nursery-school class, taking in the whole scene in a quick glance, looking for a spot to light.

A more solitary type might head straight for his favored play, looking neither to right nor left, hands at his sides. But Mr. Hailfellow picks the most active group, runs for it with arms all ready to take on his accustomed job in sand pile or block center, and joins right in. For him the specific play is unimportant, as long as he can cope with it. He is just as happy racing around the playground as he is listening to a story, singing, painting, or riding a tricycle, as long as other children are doing it with him.

There are gregarious children, however, who have favorite games. They don't always play with a group. A four-year-old might like to use the horizontal ladder. He might invite someone else to play with him, but if the friend refused, he'd play alone.

Some children flit quickly from one activity to another. Others get deeply involved in whatever they start first and don't like to stop until they are finished.

One group of children may be good direction followers. They will do whatever teacher says, whether it means playing alone or with a group, for a short period or a long one; whether it involves sitting, running, listening, or doing.

Other youngsters are always in motion and hardly hear suggestions. Games that demand constant running and jumping don't tire them, but they quickly get restless and inattentive when they have to sit still.

Counterparts of these children are the quiet ones who sit for hours listening to stories, playing records, or crayoning. In rough-house play they look uncomfortable and soon drop out.

All these many different styles of play are normal. However, that doesn't always make them advisable or even permissible. Sometimes good judgment, common sense, or a factor as specific as a parent's wishes may dictate that a child modify or change his ways.

Nicky's father and mother, for example, believed he should broaden his horizons. They felt that whether he ended up an engineering genius or not, he would be a sad character if he didn't learn the rewards and responsibilities of friendship. They also felt that no matter how special his interests, he had the same obligation as anyone else to abide by the rules of the group he was in. They saw to it, therefore, that he sometimes played other boys' games and went to their houses, instead of always letting them come after him. They began to be firmer about promptness at meals and about doing his share of household work.

Children who are rough sometimes need curbing. When quick, energetic, very active Rob adds a big block to the high block tower on the roof, the whole structure crashes on Jimmy, kneeling nearby. When he grabs Suzy's paintbrush because he needs her color "right away," Suzy gets stuck in the eye. Rob didn't mean it, but he must learn to be careful.

Persistent Janey rides the tricycle all morning no matter how many other children want it. She has to learn about taking turns, and she may also discover the fun of trying different things in the process.

Masterful George is much too difficult when he isn't bossing a game that involves most of the group. He'll knock people's buildings down, pull the covers off the doll beds, turn the phonograph off—anything to try to get people to stop what they're doing and play his way.

The "slow warmer-up," described in Chapter 13, is another child who sometimes needs to modify his pattern. Often he is just starting to play when the game is over, the class finished, or the party ready to break up. Parents and teachers can work on ways to make him get involved more easily and more quickly. For example, if the youngster is going to a birthday party, his mother can take him a little early and arrange with the hostess to involve him in the preparations—setting the places at the table, bringing in the games to be used, helping in cleaning up the room. By the time the other children arrive his warm-up period will be over. Or if a new playmate is coming for a first visit, the youngster can be asked to make the visitor feel at home by showing him his toys and games and explaining them. By this time the ice will be broken. With a little planning of this kind the "slow warmer-up" can be helped over his initial hump with most new situations.

There is a great difference between the normal kind of over-exuberant, one-sided play that may need to be curbed or modified at times, and the play that points to some disturbance in the child. Play reflects a child's individual temperament or style and there-fore exposes weaknesses as well as strengths. In fact, a parent or relative may get his first inkling of trouble from noticing changes in a child's play. It is always wise to get professional advice when this happens. What is abnormal play?

There are children who are afraid to join a group. They stand on the edge and worry about whether other children want them. They are not like the "slow warmer-up," who also stands on the edge at first, even when not afraid. These children look scared. They cry and cling to their mothers. If the group is playing ring-around-a-rosy, for example, and then changes to London Bridge, the fright-ened ones drop out. In fact, they usually run away whenever play takes an unpredictable turn.

A child who, even at five, won't play at another child's house may be excessively fearful. So is the one who plays alone under any circumstances. A child who grabs all the toys he can gather and refuses to let anyone else play with him or use the toys is also behaving in a disturbed fashion.

Many children are aggressive and rough in their play. However, it is not normal for a child to bristle whenever someone touches him in passing or shows affection. Nor is it a good sign when a child fights most of the day.

Some children have lots of good ideas and are very persistent, but when a child can never accept anyone else's ideas and can't stand having his wishes frustrated, his reaction is abnormal.

Some children let off steam by knocking down other people's

play—destroying block cities, smearing paintings, or stepping on sand castles. Every child has mischievous moments, but when a child's principal pleasure comes from interfering with other children's play, parents should be concerned.

Some children are overambitious and try to go way beyond their capacities. The six-year-old may insist on playing with a chemistry set; the seven-year-old may demand to be the pitcher on the Little League team. Such overambitiousness may be the result of pressures from the parents. A father who insists that his boy be a star athlete, or a mother who dreams of her son's being a Nobel Prize winner, may intrude on the child's play and try to make him conform to their ambitions.

Sometimes disturbance shows up less dramatically. A child might play in a way completely below his age and level of development. If the play has no functional meaning this may be a sign of disturbed development. It would not be normal for a three-year-old to play only with a box containing unrelated objects which he kept taking out and putting back. Monotonous repetition of the same motion or game may also be a worrisome symptom. It would be strange for a four-year-old, for instance, to roll a toy car endlessly back and forth, without ever taking it to the garage, picking up a passenger, or doing any of the thousand and one things that children normally do in imitating life with their play. One would suspect something wrong if a nursery-school child stayed at the sink all morning simply emptying and filling a bottle over and over, and never played with other children.

When a child clings compulsively to an imaginary playmate or animal after the age of six, it may be a sign of inner turmoil. One emotionally ill ten-year-old talked to us endlessly about a live squirrel that lived with him. The squirrel turned out to be a very worn stuffed animal. Even when the child brought it to show us, however, he insisted that it was alive and attacked us for not sharing his belief.

There are many highly active children who are entirely normal, but there is a clear line between normal and abnormal hyperactivity. The disturbed child not infrequently does a lot more running around *without any goal*. He doesn't seem to pay attention to the rules of a game. If he joins a running game, he doesn't seem to know when to stop, but gets more and more excited, running around, hitting other children at random, and ignoring the point of the game completely.

Lots of children despair temporarily when they don't do well. When a child strikes out at bat or misses a fly or gets clobbered at checkers, he may cry a little, accuse the other fellow of making him lose, or say, "You cheated." But the hurt should soon be over, and he should quickly go back to the game. There *are* children, however, who are destroyed when they lose or make a mistake. They run away and hide, have a tantrum, or start attacking with fists or fingernails. Such a sore loser may need help.

Since play is the child's attempt to imitate life, master his own body and mind, and learn how to cope with his world, it should show progressive sophistication, skill, and variety. If, instead, it gets narrower and narrower, and more and more antisocial, solitary, or destructive, clearly something is wrong, and it is important not to delay finding out what it is.

16 A NEW BABY ARRIVES

For most parents the second child is so much easier than the first that there is a saying, "Every first child should be a second baby." But for the older child, the arrival of a brother or sister is quite a different experience. This is the first time *he* has coped with a baby. The new baby's effect on him will depend on his age, whether he is the first child or not, his previous experience with other people's new babies, the kind of child he is, and the way his parents and grandparents treat him.

The professional literature has, in the main, emphasized the disturbing effect of a new baby's arrival on the older child. As the children (siblings) grow older, it is also usually assumed that they will become rivals for the mother's attention and develop the well-known "sibling rivalry." A leading child analyst describes the clash of a child with his brother or sister: "Jealousy and rivalry . . . now come to a climax in a final contest for a favored position with the mother; the inevitable failure leads to resignation, guilt and anxiety." [1]

There is no doubt that sibling rivalry is a fact of life in many families. The first child may express pain and even intense distress at being suddenly and unequivocally removed from number-one spot in the child-centered American home, to become just one of the children. He may protest violently when the second baby occupies his crib, uses his high chair, is fed while he is left to feed himself, and more important perhaps, takes a lot of the mother's time and attention that used to be all his.

The possibility that the new baby may also be a source of satisfaction and pleasure to the older child, unfortunately, gets little attention in most psychiatric and psychological writings. Psychiatrists and psychologists do not usually see the child who has reacted positively. But these positive responses are as meaningful as the disturbances. Once the first child is the older brother, he may enjoy being a big boy and begin to behave like older children he has watched. He may try harder to feed and dress himself. He may want to get out of a crib and into a big bed. Watching the baby so he won't fall off the bathinet, or getting powder or diapers for his mother, may make him feel important and grown-up.

In our own research study, new babies were born in a number of families in which we were already following an older child's development. This gave us an opportunity to study the older child's reaction to the arrival of the new baby. We found a wide variety of individual reactions among the children, ranging from a strong welcome to the new baby, mild positive interest, outward lack of interest, mild and short-lived distress, to rather prolonged and intense disturbance. Children in the last category, the only ones with substantial distress, were in a small minority—less than one-fifth of the group as a whole.

The positive responses of some of the children were quite striking.

Three-year-old David watched his mother changing three-week-old Gerry's diapers and announced solemnly, "I'm a big boy. I can put my own pants on." He insisted on being shown how to tell front from back and how to lay his pants out on the bed so he could step into them correctly. At first he had trouble getting each foot into a different pants leg, but he tried patiently until he was successful. When visitors arrived, David proudly announced, "I can put my pants on all by myself," and was roundly praised.

Susie at twenty months was being toilet trained and had achieved partial bladder control. Approximately three-quarters of the time she would use the toilet; the rest of the time she had accidents. With the arrival of Jimmy, she showed an active interest in the fact that he wet himself and had to stay wet until someone changed him. With each diaper change Susie went to sit on her potty seat and would return to report, "I did a big wee-wee" or "I did a little wee-wee."

Arnie at age four was still not feeding himself. He watched his mother spoon-feed Pablum to his baby sister. Several days later he announced, "I eat all by myself" and refused to let his mother or grandmother feed him.

As might have been expected, a new baby caused more upsets in first children than in second or third children. The younger children, those under eighteen months, reacted less, either positively or negatively, than did the older ones.

The father's relationship to the child also made a difference. In several families, the father had taken an active part in the care of the youngster from birth on. He continued this after the birth of the new baby, and this seemed to cushion the effects of losing some of the mother's attention.

The youngsters who were by temperament quickly adaptable, mild, and positive in their responses tended to take the new baby in their stride, just as they had accepted new foods, new places, and new people outside the family. The intense, predominantly negative, and slowly adaptable child generally had more trouble accepting the new baby, in keeping with his response to other new situations.

Our findings indicate that the emotional dangers a new baby is supposed to create for his older brother or sister have frequently been exaggerated in the child-care literature. At the same time, the attention given in this literature to the issue of sibling rivalry undoubtedly has had certain beneficial results. Parents have become more alert to the possibility of jealousy when a new baby is born. They prepare for it. They sympathize with the older child's distress and accent the positive aspects of being a brother or sister.

Nowadays, a visitor at a home where there is a new baby rarely has to be warned to pay some attention to the older child before making his exclamations over the infant. He will probably even have a little gift for the first child to match his present for the smaller one. The visitor will often find that the first-born has been given a prominent role in the ceremony of introducing the newest member of the family to friends and relatives. He leads the guests to the baby's room and opens the baby's presents for him.

Parents usually make an effort to keep from jolting the first child's confidence in his place in the family. The baby's schedule is adjusted to the older child's established routines. The mother, for example, finds that she can prop a bottle for the baby to suck while she takes two-year-old Timmy to the bathroom, reads him a bed-time story, or helps him with his meal as in the past. She will shift the baby's bathtime to correspond to Timmy's naptime or another spot in the day when Timmy is busily engaged outside the house. Rarely in the enlightened household these days does one hear a mother exclaim, "Stop bothering me. Can't you see I'm feeding the baby?"

These attitudes and actions of parents, relatives, and visitors help the older child to make a smooth adjustment to the new baby. Sometimes, however, the older child is so elaborately prepared by the parent to accept the new baby as his own dear treasure and closest playmate, that he is rudely disappointed when the new baby actually arrives. When parents go overboard in their efforts to "sell" the new baby, the older child has to adjust to the fact that the new-comer is not just another stuffed animal or pull-toy, but a living, breathing thing that has to have care and attention, just the way he does.

Some parents have been made so fearful by what they have read about the dangers of sibling rivalry that they try to make the older child believe nothing has changed. They may try to smuggle the new baby into the family, trying to convince the first-born by words and actions that he is still the only important child in the household. Such behavior invites disaster. It gives the first-born a totally unreal and quite dangerous feeling of his place in the family group, and relegates the new baby to second-class citizenship. It robs the older child of the fun a baby can bring to the family and to him. A baby sister can be a wonderful audience. All Billy has to do is look at her and she smiles. If he jumps up and down, she giggles. When he runs around the room, her eyes never leave him. Soon she begins to talk. Her first or second word is "Billy," which everyone in the family notices.

Close brother-and-sister relationships do not develop in hot-house surroundings where each child is studiously shielded from the other and encouraged to feel that he can develop without acknowledging anyone else's needs or rights, or even gifts and charms. Such shielding also deprives children of the opportunities provided by the realistic give-and-take of family life for easier development of social maturity.

In the family, and especially with his brothers and sisters, the child gets his first experience with the endlessly rich and complex nature of friendship and affection. Companionship between children in a family grows as they live together, play with each other, and even fight with each other. Disputes flare up over even small issues, and rivalry and jealousy may be subtly or not so subtly intertwined with their positive feelings. The experience of working out such disagreements and rivalries without spoiling their companionship can help children as they develop other friendships.

Parents should accept their children's clashes and disputes as a fact of family life that does not necessarily have ominous significance. But parents can do much to guide sibling relationships so that the children become allied in friendly feelings and common values, rather than divided by competition and hostility.

The questions of when and how much the parents should interfere cannot be settled by a set of rules. Parents' attitudes and positions have to be modified from year to year as the issues and relationships change.

When mother takes two-month-old Allen on her lap, three-year-old Pamela tries to push him off. Mother doesn't scold or reason. She simply pulls Pamela onto her lap, too, and cuddles both children. Pamela gets a first lesson in sharing her mother with her brother. A year later when Allen is fourteen months old, he marches over and knocks down his sister's block castle. Pamela, now four, starts to hit him with a block. Mother intervenes quickly, but calmly. "Don't hit him. He doesn't know any better. He's trying to play." She adds, "Build it up again, and I'll put him in the playpen so he won't bother you."

This scene, with infinite variations, may be repeated scores of times before Pamela realizes that Allen is not *purposely* destructive and learns how to defend her rights without attacking him as an enemy.

When she is seven and he is four, Allen scribbles in her second-grade notebook. Pamela realizes that he is now old enough to know better. She hits him—not very hard. He goes crying to mother. But mother tells him to let Pamela's things alone if he doesn't want to get hit again.

Later on Pamela may try—as many older children do—to exploit her younger brother. Big brothers and sisters often send the little one on errands and give him orders. They make fun of everything he does and may not hesitate to "clobber" him if he gets in their way or steps out of line. In various ways they try out the role of despot, sometimes benevolent, sometimes tyrannical. When this happens, parents may have to step in. They can try to persuade the older child that he will get more help and cooperation from his younger brother if it is obtained willingly instead of by force. If little brother or sister is being swamped by a stream of remarks like "How can you be so dumb?" or "Can't you learn?" or "You must have holes in your head," the parents can intervene and calmly but firmly apply the brakes.

Calmness is not always easy to maintain. A parent who sees big eight-year-old Joey unmercifully smacking a helpless three-year-old brother may very well become outraged and horrified at this exhibition of brute violence. But if the parent's anger leads him to intervene on the side of the three-year-old and hit Joey back, he will only reinforce Joey's idea that superior force decides everything.

Sometimes parents have to "save" the older child from exploitation by the younger. Three-year-old Cathy cries a lot when she is playing with Mark, aged six. Mother begins to watch more closely to see what's the matter. She finds that Mark has a way of taking over everything Cathy tries to do, ostensibly to "show her how." Mother tells him to stop and tells Cathy to call her if he doesn't. Then the situation changes. Pretty soon Mark complains that Cathy is teasing. Indeed she is. She pushes herself into his games and spoils his visits with friends. When he complains, she says in typical small-sister fashion, "Mummy says you have to let me. If you don't, I'll tell on you." Now Cathy needs a rebuke.

Throughout the changing course of family experiences, friendship and love materialize. When Pamela is five, she picks two-year-old Allen up when he scrapes his knee, tries to wipe off the dirt, and helps him home to Mother to be comforted. When she is eight, she takes all her friends to see the first picture he painted in kindergarten. Sometimes she drops into his classroom during recess to see that he's happy

Joey, at ten, is overheard giving his eight-year-old brother advice on how to handle a bully. In conclusion he says, "If he tries it again, just come for me. I'll take care of him."

He shows him how to throw an inside curve, how to bunt, and proudly recounts his triumph to their father. His younger brother comes to him for help with arithmetic.

Parental understanding and patience by no means guarantee continuous brotherly love and family harmony. The so-called insatiable child—the one who always wants one more story, one more drink, one more turn on the slide—is likely to feel displaced by a new baby and make everlasting demands on his parents to show him that he is still loved. A parent might try to please such a child until all life revolved around him and still not succeed. Another parent, no less sympathetic but more objective, would set clear-cut limits from the start so that the older child would not monopolize her time and attention.

A child who has enjoyed a particular activity with his father or mother may be acutely aware of even a slight change in this activity after a baby's arrival and blame the baby. One four-year-old played "Memory" with his father every night. After the baby was born, the father had speeded up the game almost imperceptibly to give himself time to play with the baby before she went to sleep. The little boy noticed the change and tried to drag out the game by teasing. When the father realized that a ten-minute delay in bedtime for the baby wouldn't make any difference, he relaxed with his son and the teasing stopped.

The gregarious child whose pleasure comes mainly from doing things with people will be upset if his parents exclude him from helping by going for diapers or sprinkling powder or holding his little brother or sister. When the household routines change after a baby comes, the child who adapts only slowly to new experiences will obviously be harder to mollify than the eager-beaver, quickly adaptive youngster.

Fortunately, children are usually resilient. If one approach doesn't work and sibling rivalry gets out of hand, this doesn't mean the children will be permanently damaged. A shift in parental tactics, taking into account the new issues over which the children are battling, may work quickly. But the new tactics will also have to be modified as the children move on to new patterns of companionship, joint activities, and agreements and disagreements.

17 GOING TO NURSERY SCHOOL

Any attempt to weigh the need for nursery school with a middle-class audience is bound to seem academic. The nursery school has become such a well-established institution in American life that "juice time," "show and tell," "rest," "old and young threes" —once specialized terms of the nursery-school educator—are now part of the vernacular.

A middle-class city parent who would prefer not to send his child to nursery school often faces the fact that the youngster will have trouble finding playmates. All the other three-year-olds on the block will be off to school at 8:30 sharp. Most of them return in midafternoon in no condition for a new round of fun and games.

In many neighborhoods, then, nursery school is almost a practical necessity if children are to have regular companionship with other boys and girls before they go to kindergarten. It is also a great convenience. Mothers who work feel much easier when they know that their children are in a good school and stop worrying about whether the nurse or housekeeper is affectionate and reliable and intelligent enough to take their place. Mothers who stay at home find that nursery school allows them some free time to pick up the interests they set aside when the baby came, as well as more time for the younger children, for rest, or simply for the never-finished round of household work and errands.

Parents also generally believe that nursery school provides valuable experience that will help their children academically and socially when they enter first grade. Certain parents become frantic about getting a child into one of the "best" nursery schools as an essential first hike up the long ladder to Harvard or Radcliffe—fifteen years hence.

Actually, children can learn a great deal in nursery school. They use blocks—first to build such simple and familiar structures as skyscrapers, but finally to construct entire cities, complete with electric wiring, street signs, billboards, subway tunnels, and so on. In the sandbox their play introduces them to all kinds of physical laws. They learn about leverage and the powers of the pulley. They figure out how electricity works and the meaning of weight, volume, and balance. They get their first glimmerings of mathematical concepts by following recipes for applesauce or vegetable soup, or by taking attendance day by day. They learn to recognize similarities and distinguish differences, which may help in learning to read. They may even learn to make letters, label their pictures, and even write illustrated stories with their teachers' help.

Dolls, household tools, vehicles with wheels, and climbing equipment stimulate their imaginations and exercise their fast-growing muscles. Little personal closets for their things help them learn to take care of what's theirs and to recognize what is someone else's. The day's play provides lesson after lesson in becoming a social human being. It is also good preparation for moving smoothly into first grade.

But the underprivileged children who could benefit most from nursery school are the ones least likely to get there. What nursery school has to offer the child of an economically and culturally privileged background is in large part also available in his home, which probably boasts a fair complement of nursery-school materials, including the indispensable easel with poster paints and large brushes and stacks of newsprint to encourage creative profligacy in the young.

In the enlightened mother and father the child has teachers as enthusiastic if less objective and trained than those he would encounter in school. If their own childhood was a happy one, these parents eagerly anticipate seeing their children repeat their own early experiences. If they view their own early years as deprived ones, they are determined that their own children will have a better start in life.

Not only do such parents supply a rich and sometimes extravagant array of toys and materials, but they also plan trips to zoos, museums, and firehouses, tell stories, read books, stimulate curiosity, and welcome questions.

What the home may not be able to provide as well as a good nursery school does are social experiences, lessons in sharing, in cooperation, in self-assertion, and in self-defense. The school situation offers more opportunities for the child to learn to work and play with others who have different attitudes and points of view. However, these advantages in social learning of the nursery-school experience are not necessarily crucial. Our research study has found that the children from middle-class homes who went to nursery school at three had a more active level of social functioning at school the following year when compared with the children coming into school for the first time at four years. However, by kindergarten, this advantage over children who had had less or even no preschool experience disappeared. The child starting school at three years may have an earlier social development as compared with the normal middle-class stay-at-home youngster, but the latter tends to catch up by the age of five or six.

Nursery school may have much more important advantages for the slum-raised child who comes from a home that may be seriously deficient in the kinds of enriching experiences that prepare children's eyes, ears, hands, and minds for academic learning in the first grades. Nursery schools for such deprived children are desirable to help overcome deficiencies in their home experiences. A number of cities have begun such programs, and the Federal Government is now also beginning to support them.

Whether children are from privileged or deprived segments of the population, those who do not adapt easily to new experiences and new people will get particular benefit from nursery school. These children, who are described in Chapters 13 and 14, need as many positive experiences as they can get in meeting and playing with other children, taking directions and accommodating themselves to the requirements of the classroom and playground. Such experiences will help them to adjust more easily to group life and learning when they reach first grade. In addition, the child who has no brothers or sisters gets special pleasure and stimulation from nursery-school life.

While the expressed aim of a good nursery school is to develop the child's *individual* capacities, it does not always escape the influence of conventional values and stereotypes. A child's success is not always measured in terms of his individual progress, but sometimes by his approximation to the cultural norm: "outward-directed," "task-oriented," "group-minded."

This same standard is not infrequently used in judging the child's acceptability for a nursery school. The young applicant is frequently ushered into a deserted classroom, first by himself, and then perhaps with a group of fellow applicants, and his behavior observed. There are materials: sand, water, clay, paint, blocks; some equipment: furnishings, dolls, animals, trucks, wagons, etc.; and a pet or two: guinea pig, hamster, white rat, parakeet, turtle, fish. The child's responses are watched and weighed. Ideally, he will love the furry animals and show no fear of them, be curious about fish and turtles, utilize almost all the materials, and engage in conversation and even active play (if he's turned three) with the other youngsters and the teachers. In short, he will be a gregarious, fairly verbal, curious, active, friendly, warm, positive child.

Nursery-school teachers and parents know—when they stop to think—that many healthy children don't come close to fitting this stereotype and never will. To use it as the standard of measurement for healthy behavior runs completely counter to an educational program dedicated to *developing* the *individual* child. The assumption that all children will adjust in the same way and behave alike in school denies the individuality of their personalities.

Many schools also anticipate that most children will have a hard time leaving their mothers. Often elaborate rituals are established to ease the separation. Sometimes months may pass before the child is finally judged "ready" to be alone in school for a full day without his mother. It is almost universal for schools to expect mothers to be prepared to stay for the first week.

It seems sensible for a school to let the mother participate with it in judging what will suit her child. If children are individuals there can be no *one* best way to leave mother. What is best is what is best for a particular child, and the mother is often in a fine position to contribute information on what has been found to be best.

Many youngsters view the prospect of going to school with keen anticipation. They walk into nursery school the first day with never a look backward. If they have had a preliminary visit or two and gotten to know the teacher, they don't need their mothers to stay. They don't need to work up gradually to a full day's stay. These are the easily adaptable children with predominantly positive mood and approach reactions. They are ready to pitch in. Nothing will happen if their mothers stay; they just won't pay much attention to them. They will be too busy investigating all the new things to do, people to play with, and adults to talk to. The excitement of all the novelty and variety absorbs them quickly and completely. Even certain children who otherwise might not be easily adaptable also move in quickly because they have older brothers and sisters whom they have watched in school.

Three-year-old Allen moved into nursery school the first day with this kind of zest. He made a dash into the classroom, began playing with the other children there, and then turned to his mother in a puzzled way and asked, "Why don't you go home?"

His mother was startled. She had read again and again about the emotional trauma of first separation; she had been told by the nursery school to stay for the first two weeks, and she had arranged her schedule accordingly. Yet here was Allen telling her to go home after his first five minutes in school. Did he really mean it, or would he feel deserted by her if she left? Not knowing what to do, she stayed the morning, completely ignored by Allen until it was time for him to go home. She called us for advice that afternoon. We reminded her that Allen had plunged into almost all new situations in this same positive fashion since early infancy. There was every reason to believe that he didn't need her at school. And so it turned out. She left him every day at the bus; he went cheerfully, participated happily in school, and never asked for her.

There are many children who may not embrace the new nursery-school experience immediately for a number of reasons. The child who, in general, warms up slowly to new situations will adapt more easily if his mother stays on during the first days while he is still sorting out the classroom, the equipment, and the population. He may not *seem* to be relying on his mother's presence as he gingerly approaches the sandbox or pushes a truck over to another boy's garage, but he depends on her, and if she leaves before he is ready, he will often retreat to the side lines with a toy he's brought from home. For this kind of child the nursery-school plan for mother to stay for two weeks may be exactly right.

Some children who seem to want their mothers most, often do better without them. They are children who show a one-track attitude toward life very early. For example, if they are taken to a certain restaurant for lunch one day and eat a chicken sandwich and a chocolate soda, they will always order that lunch and want to go to that restaurant. If they get a balloon from the barber with their first haircut, they'll hold out a hand for a balloon at the same moment on the second visit. If their mother stays with them in nursery school on the first few days, they will expect her to be there every day.

If the one-track child is also the kind who adapts easily to new surroundings, he will adapt quickly to nursery school and to the fact that his mother is not there. In fact, if she does at first stay, he may feel threatened and quite rebellious when she does try to leave.

Nina was one such youngster. Her mother stayed with her the first few days, and nursery school then became for her a place where mother comes and stays while you play with other children. If her mother had left her the first day, nursery school would just as easily have been the place where mother brings you and goes home while you stay and play with other children.

Nina made a considerable commotion when her mother finally did leave after the first week. Mother worried and so did the nursery-school teacher. Did this mean that Nina was actually an insecure child who needed her mother's presence for a longer period of time? Our study records indicated no evidence of any such insecurity in the girl. The next day her mother left her again at school. Nina's commotion the second day was very brief. Within a few minutes after her mother left Nina was playing happily. Nursery school now became the place where she went happily without her mother so she could play with her friends.

A few children use their mother's presence to turn school into a home away from home. They insist on playing with their mother and ignore the teacher and the other children. This is sometimes a sign of psychological difficulty in the child or the mother which should be explored by competent specialists before any final decision about continuing school is made.

If a child always has trouble leaving his mother when she goes to shop or takes him to play with a friend or for a visit with a relative, she can predict that she will be needed during the first days of school. If the child does not make any overtures toward playthings or children while she is there, she should try leaving him alone. Even if he protests vehemently it might be wise to continue the experiment for several days. If this does not work, there are additional ways of making the adjustment easier. The father might take the child to school to see whether the youngster can part with him more smoothly. The teacher can make special efforts to act as a substitute for mother. The mother might leave the youngster very briefly at first, and the length of time she leaves be stepped up gradually.

In most cases the protests dwindle to token resistance in a week or so, and the child gradually becomes a full, active member of the group.

Some children, however, continue to be miserable after the first week, spending most of the day crying, fighting, or sucking their thumbs in solitude. They are probably not mature enough for school. Consultation with a pediatrician or psychiatrist might bring out ways to help them develop more confidence and independence.

Many adults, though sincerely believing in cultivating individuality, succumb to stereotyped thinking about children. Just as many teachers and parents, too, expect all children to adapt to nursery school in more or less uniform fashion, they also expect them to behave the same way once they've fitted in, and assume something is wrong when they don't. Sociability and active energetic play are commonly attributed to healthy self-confidence. Gentleness and capacity to enjoy solitary play are laid to fearfulness.

Actually, there are children for whom solitary play may be normal. Ronnie, one of our study children, was always just as happy playing alone as with a friend or group. He often chose to play alone, but was friendly if others joined him as long as they didn't interfere with his puzzle or block structure. He was not a behavior problem. As an adult, he will probably enjoy solitary pursuits.

Teachers sometimes describe a child as anxious because he doesn't participate actively enough in music or dancing and seems slow to join group activities. But we have found that some of these children, too, are not fearful, but rather slow warmers-up. When we reviewed the children's records with their parents and pointed out the similarity of the nursery-school adjustment to other experiences, they relaxed. They were able to wait out the child's period of limited participation. Eventually the children found their place in the nursery-school group, chose the activities they liked, and convinced their teachers that they were normal.

Another type of child who is sometimes mislabeled anxious in nursery school is the one with selective interests. For example, Elsie's parents were told that during running games she always withdrew to the side lines and refused to participate. The teacher suggested, "Maybe she is anxious." But the parents knew that Elsie was usually very clear-cut and selective in her interests. If she liked a new food or game or person, she showed this very openly. Her negative reactions were just as definite and open and hard to change. They suggested to the teacher, "Let's ask Elsie why she doesn't play tag." Elsie's reply was characteristic: "I don't like running games. I'm happier when I just stand and watch them."

It is not always so easy to protect parents and children from the faulty diagnoses of overunderstanding friends, relatives, and teachers. Perhaps the best security is the constant reminder that children are different. Good nursery-school directors and teachers do not try to fit children with arbitrary labels. They are often very helpful in reassuring a worried, inexperienced parent that her child's behavior is really normal even though it is different from the other children's.

Youngsters also remain different as they go on in school. We have followed the 136 middle-class children in our study through nursery school, into kindergarten and elementary school. Their behavior continues to differ as they go along in school. These differences reflect fundamental styles of behavior just as clearly as the ways the children reacted to food, strangers, or toys when they were babies.

Some children approach new games more actively and energetically than others. They experiment and explore and adventure more. Some are very hesitant and slow to explore. They stay on the side lines a lot until they have had time to decide what they like. Some children are more interested in people and seldom play alone. Others are more interested in the task they are doing and can be happy playing alone or with others. Some are more active, some more distractible, some more persistent, some more intense.

One way of behaving is not intrinsically better or worse than another, nor does it signify better or worse parental care. However, one may be more convenient for teachers, more fun for children, or even easier for the child himself. In the child's own interest, therefore, parents and teachers may try to guide children so that reaction characteristics do not interfere with successful functioning. They might, for example, try to give a child who adapts to changes and innovations with difficulty many opportunities to discover how easy changes and new things can be. Or a teacher might foresee learning difficulties for the distractible child who flits from one activity to another without ever concentrating long at anything, and try to get him so involved in one activity that he works hard, concentrates, and enjoys the pleasure of seeing his finished work. Enough such lessons will make it easier for him to settle down in first grade, where learning becomes a more essential part of the school day.

Susie is a child who almost always works alone. She has a strong creative bent and paints, works with clay, saws, hammers, and builds things all day long. Her teacher doesn't expect or want to turn her into a group leader, but she recognizes the virtue of Susie's learning to get along with other children, and so she looks for natural opportunities to involve her with them.

The doll cradle breaks and Susie is asked to repair it. When she finishes, she accepts the invitation to play house with the homemaker group. At Christmas the class plans a mural and Susie joins in enthusiastically. When the girls continue talking about their painting during outdoor play, Susie goes on talking and playing with them. Gradually friends become important to her.

This kind of effort to modify a child's characteristics so that he can get along better with people and find more success and satisfaction in his life and work can be helpful to a child. It is a far cry from setting up the all-American boy and girl as the model for all children and trying to bend each boy and girl to it. Fortunately, most teachers, and parents as well, are too perceptive and sensitive to be trapped by such stereotyped thinking.

18 LEARNING IN STYLE

Children learn formal school subjects differently, whether reading, arithmetic, science, or foreign languages. These differences have many causes, such as intellectual level, special aptitudes and talents, motivation for learning, the attitudes of the parents, and the stimulation provided by the home environment. These issues have been studied extensively. The facts of their influence on the child's formal learning are fairly general knowledge and will not be repeated here.

Less well known is the importance of the child's temperament in the learning process. Our study has revealed a great deal about how children with different temperaments react to formal learning.

The persistent baby who kept trying over and over to drink from his cup even when he kept spilling almost all the milk, and who practiced tying his shoelaces for an hour or more at a time, frequently displayed the same tenacious attitude toward learning to read.

The toddler who put on one shoe, then saw a block that needed replacing on his barn; put on another shoe, then looked out the window; went to his mother to get his shoes tied, but saw the cat and stopped to pat him on the way—in a word, the more distractible child with short attention span—got his lessons learned, too, but in brief frequent sessions.

The youngster who made friends easily with strangers and never wanted to play alone sometimes got sidetracked when there were too many classroom opportunities for being social.

The intense, predominantly negative little boy who at three and a half got on his tricycle, made one effort to apply pressure to the pedals, and then fell off, sobbing in despair, sometimes had a frustrating time in first grade, but with a patient, encouraging teacher he learned just as successfully as he had finally learned to ride his tricycle.

The mildly active baby who sat quietly in his high chair and never splashed vigorously in his bath did not have trouble sitting still in class. The highly active toddler who wriggled in his high chair long before his meal was over and always preferred running to walking sometimes became the restless first-grader who was constantly finding excuses to leave his seat.

But every child—assuming normal intelligence—can master the demands of school when his own individual approach to learning is recognized and enlisted positively by his parents at home and his teachers at school.

These days the recognition of children's individual learning styles is more important then ever before. Higher education holds the key to interesting jobs, financial success, and social status. The school drop-out faces a dismal future. Parent and school pressure on children for academic achievement is mounting. Earlier starts in formal learning are recommended by a number of education experts, who believe that the normal three- or four-year-old can be taught reading and mathematics. These demands for expanded and early learning can be a constructive and stimulating challenge to the child if they are appropriate to his intellectual level and his individual style of learning. When they are not, however, they can lead to student disaffection, underachievement, and school dropout.

A youngster's preschool years offer many opportunities to observe his individual learning style. A child's first months and years are full of learning experiences. From watching the way children tackle these early challenges a good deal can be predicted about how they will behave when they get to school. This insight can be used for guiding the child so that his first formal learning experiences will be constructive ones and will set a positive attitude to learning that can carry through school.

The highly adaptable child with predominantly positive mood can be expected to approach school and formal learning the same way as he did most new situations. He usually can adapt successfully and quickly to different academic approaches whether permissive or highly structured.

This was true of Carol, who moved as smoothly into first grade as she had into a new neighborhood, into nursery school, and into kindergarten. She was a first-class direction follower. All lessons were done neatly and conformed exactly to the teacher's instructions. Whether it was pasting pictures in her notebook to illustrate letters of the alphabet or writing out spelling words three times each, all assignments were done carefully and punctually. She also worked productively when given leeway in doing a topic as thoroughly as she wanted. Each topic aroused her enthusiastic interest and stimulated animated discussion with her parents and older brother.

The easy child, however, may also have his problems, depending on the parents and the school. He may have adapted very easily at home to parental expectations and desires which then make school difficult for him. The girl Pammy, described under "The Easy Child" in Chapter 4, is a good example of this sequence. Also, if the school is narrow and rigid in its approach, he may adapt all too well, and his own interests and special intellectual talents may never be expressed.

Gary started in such a school with a pedantic and mechanical approach to learning. In his preschool years he had shown a wide-ranging curiosity in everything he noticed and always had a new "why" to bring to his parents: "Why is the moon out at night?" "Why does a piano make a different sound from a violin?" "Why does a dog walk on four legs instead of two?" His parents were delighted with his questions, answered them enthusiastically, and encouraged him to ask more—which he did. All this changed after Gary started school. He enjoyed going, learned the classroom routines without difficulty, and did all his assigned work conscientiously. But his stream of questions at home dried up completely. And when his parents tried to discuss his school work with him he answered, "We're not supposed to do that. My teacher says we should learn only from her, and nobody at home should help us." Gary, a very adaptable child in everything, had now adapted as quickly to the school environment and demands as he had done previously to the atmosphere at home.

The difficult child who tends to be intensely negative in his first reactions to people, places, and things might be expected to have trouble in adjusting in school, and many do. However, this is far from universally true. Several such children we are following in the study are doing very well. They have even become enthusiastic students.

Parents play a crucial role in the outcome. A father or mother who is frightened of the possible effects of pushing a child to do something he doesn't like will shield the persistently negative youngster from exposure to new experiences. A parent who pushes too fast and too hard or vacillates between pushing and protection will make new experiences unpleasant for such a child. Nothing could be less helpful than these approaches. What the youngster needs is enough experience in strange situations, under good auspices, to find out that learning is not bad after all.

Among the difficult children in our study, the ones who were carefully taught in the preschool years to apply themselves to new tasks until they finally experienced the rewards, settled down in first grade fairly quickly. One typical example was Willie, whose mother had learned to patiently wait out his first negative reactions to anything new. When he started school, she briefed the teacher on what to expect. She was sure Willie would be difficult at first, but she was just as sure he would settle down if the teacher quietly but firmly repeated the rules to him each day. The teacher took her cue from this mother, who really seemed to know her child. Within a month Willie's initial difficult phase was past, and he soon became a superior and imaginative student.

In contrast, the protected or pressured negative children generally became school problems. Susan, one such child, had impatient but inconsistent parents who alternately pressured and vacillated. She became more negative and resistant to even simple requests. When she started school, resistance to obeying the routine school rules became an increasing problem. She was so busy battling the teacher that she could not apply herself to learning. Though she was a bright child, her progress in school was retarded. Psychiatric treatment became necessary to prevent her from developing a serious learning problem.

The nonpersistent child with a short attention span usually is also easily distractible and less intensely involved in whatever he is doing. Whether mastering the baking of mud pies or the concepts of algebra, he learns by fits and starts. At twelve months he may try to feed his Pablum to himself, but after a few tries he gives up the experiment for the day. The next lesson will be just as brief. Then a few days later he may pick up the spoon and use it quite efficiently. He often seems to learn while his back is turned.

If such a child has parents who aren't in any more hurry than he is, he will progress smoothly. When he is ready for first grade, a school where classes are short and lessons brief will exactly suit his way of learning in small doses. Pressed to learn faster by concentrating for longer periods than are natural for him, he may become balky and upset, and even completely lose interest in learning.

At home this same child will get more out of his work if he learns to plan his study time to fit his way of learning. It is useless, for example, to insist that he stay at a task until he has mastered it if this will require hours of concentration. He will learn more quickly and establish better work habits if, instead, he tackles his work in several short periods.

The persistent child often seems to be made for learning. Parents and teachers usually have only to use a light guiding hand to keep him chugging along in his steady and often dedicated effort to learn whatever is put before him.

When he started to learn to feed himself, he didn't give up until he could get food from plate to mouth in one easy motion. When he got a tricycle, he spent all of his time outdoors practicing back and forth and around until he could handle it like a veteran. When he saw his older brother doing homework, he began doing homework too. As fast as his brother would give him words to write and read, or numbers to learn, he would get to work at them and stick to it until he had mastered them all.

Nothing will interfere with this kind of child's continuing his highly focused course through school except frustration of his efforts. The persistent child does not always cooperate in what his teacher has planned. If he has not finished his arithmetic when arithmetic class is over, for example, he may keep right on plugging away at his sums while the rest of the class is getting ready for gym. The patient teacher can wait and persuade: "We're through with arithmetic now, Harry. You can go back to that problem in your free time." Often, however, patience and time are at a premium in busy schools. The teacher's reaction is just as likely to be exasperation. Too many exasperated teachers will dampen even the persistent child's thirst for knowledge.

Trying to make the intense, involved child who never gets tired of doing what interests him into a model student persisting just the right amount in every class at school and on every task at home would frustrate his natural interest in learning to the point where he might not do anything well, or change him from a serious and perhaps highly creative student in his field of special interest, to a run-of-the-mill good performer. But parents and teachers can usually win such a child's cooperation if they acknowledge and respect his interests, help satisfy them, and hold demands for general school performance to reasonable limits.

With a four-year-old, for example, it helps to establish a definite end for an activity that is hard to put down. "We're going out in ten minutes. Put the sky and the sun in your picture and you can do the flowers when you get back."

If trouble develops over the completion of homework, a father might suggest that a child with one consuming interest do his other subjects first and then spend all his remaining time on his favorite work.

The three-year-old who drops his head to one side, moves closer to his mother, and then freezes at the entrance to a strange room full of strange people will not master the routines and the lessons of first grade as fast as the more outgoing child who might not even have paused on the threshold. Many parents get so used to the slow, steady way this kind of child tucks away all kinds of information and experience that they may not be prepared for his first reaction to school. A little foresight can prevent a great deal of trouble. Arranging several casual and short preliminary visits to the school and classroom he'll be in, and later establishing the habit of going over lessons at home with him regularly if it can be done in a relaxed atmosphere, will make the introduction to learning smoother. The slow starter often needs more practice with letters, sounds, words, numbers, and ideas, just as he needs more exposure to new people, new foods, and new places before he can make himself at home with them.

He can be discouraged easily by impatient teachers. When he has to move ahead to new lessons before he's secure in his mastery of the old ones, he may feel confused and frustrated. Parents can step in at such times and help him keep up with new material he gets at school.

Teachers often revise their first impression when they have a chance to see the quality of performance such a child is capable of in time, but it can make school easier for the child if a parent describes his way of approaching things to the teacher at the beginning of the term.

Annie, a child in our study who was slow to warm up, attended an experimental program of accelerating selected first-graders. On the basis of her performance in first grade she was included in a group who were to do second- and third-grade work in a single year. After several weeks in this new class the teacher called Annie's mother in for a discussion. The teacher felt Annie could not cope with this special class. The youngster was very quiet, never volunteered, and her work was frequently incomplete or incorrect. The teacher thought Annie would be much better off transferred to the less demanding regular class. The mother informed the teacher that this was typical of Annie's first reaction to everything new. She was sure that if the teacher was patient Annie would soon begin to move into high gear. In the spring the teacher told this story to our staff interviewer. She confessed that she had thought Annie's mother was fooling herself. But the mother really knew her child. Annie had soon begun to participate, her work improved steadily, and she ended the year very successfully.

It's much easier for the child who likes to sit still and work quietly to get adjusted to school than it is for the one who does a lot of bouncing up and down and running around. However, good schools take these differences into account in arranging the day's plans. Teachers size up the children and give the more active ones some extra room in which to breathe. Even when the group is large, the skillful teacher will give the active child more work at the board, more errands to do, more chance to use his muscles. She will also try to avoid blanket demands on the class as a whole for absolute silence and immobility.

Most active children will gradually settle down in school as their interest and involvement in work deepen. The more their interest is stimulated, the easier it will be for them to sit still, pay attention, and learn. If they are punished for every squirm and wiggle, doodle and poke as first-graders, school quickly becomes disagreeable, and it is increasingly hard to persuade them that learning is worth-while.

However, the highly active child should not be protected from the normal demands of a typical school day. If he is allowed so much leeway that he turns school into an extended play period, he will not learn to accept school work as necessary and desirable. Without gradual, systematic training in the work of learning, his entire educational progress may be jeopardized.

This happened to Billy. In nursery school his great energy and almost constant movement made him a handful to manage. At the same time he was cheerful, cooperative, and bright, and the teachers and other children made allowances for him. In the first and second grade his teachers again found him an attractive youngster. They hoped that his restlessness and difficulty in sitting still would disappear if he could "use up" his extra energy. Being in a small permissive school, they let him run up and down the halls and up and down the stairs whenever he wanted. But he did not settle down with this regime. On the contrary, school became a place to romp around. He learned little, and by the end of the second grade he was already significantly below his age level in reading. The school also began to lose patience with his behavior. On our advice the parents transferred him to a more traditional school where rules of proper school behavior were patiently but clearly set for him. He was very restless and fidgety at first, but quickly began to be absorbed in the learning situation. His academic achievement rose quickly. He began to limit the time, place, and circumstances of his playing and could sit almost as quietly as most of the children.

Some children are "task oriented"; they focus primarily on the job to be done. Relationships with people, while important and enjoyable to them, do not take first place in their interests. They do well with school tasks as long as parents and teachers do not worry and press them to be the stereotyped outgoing, gregarious youngster.

Occasionally a task-oriented and persistent child becomes a learning problem if he concentrates too much on the tasks of his own choosing. This happened to Jimmy, who was always fascinated by numbers and mathematical procedures from his preschool days on. As he went on in school he always did extraordinarily well in mathematics but fell behind in other subjects. It became necessary to teach him to be more responsive to people and their demands. Only then could he really be aware of what the teacher wanted him to do and turn his attention to all his school subjects.

By contrast, other children respond more to the person than to the task. We call them "person oriented." These were the babies who smiled quickly at a human face, whether familiar or strange. Unlike some infants who played in their playpens oblivious of what was happening around them, they would reach up to be held as soon as anyone came into their line of vision.

The person-oriented child usually has no trouble fitting in socially in school. He tends to make friends easily with the teacher and his classmates. His danger is that he may learn primarily to please his teacher and not for the sake of the lesson itself. If he doesn't like the teacher, he may say, "I'm not going to work for him. He's a heel." Parents should avoid using the time-honored ploy, "Don't you want to make that work look neater to please your teacher?" to prod the sociable child. It may encourage a tendency to work only to please. Such a child needs to recognize that learning can also be for his own interest and advantage, rather than only an additional bridge to personal relationships with teachers or other children. A teacher who has a businesslike approach to learning will be more helpful to him than one who always tries to make learning fun and a game.

Certain other aspects of learning style warrant brief mention. Some children learn in pieces. Some learn in wholes. The child who learns to swing by practicing one push at a time, before putting them all together to "pump," is a piecemeal learner. He learns to ride a bicycle in the same step-by-step fashion. The child who takes the entire swinging process as one whole unit and then gets on the swing and swings, learns in wholes. He will learn to ride a bike the same way, in toto, without breaking the process down into single steps. The first child will usually memorize tables, dates, and details of methods with little trouble. The second child usually can't memorize isolated facts very well until he understands the significance of the whole block of learning he's mastering. Both children can learn effectively if the teaching process takes into account their individual styles.

Some children have visual memories and learn by seeing. Some have auditory memories; they learn by remembering sounds. Some learn physically. The very act of forming letters and words with their lips and hands helps plant them in their minds. Good schools take these differences into account by using a combination of different approaches. In reading, for example, they use phonics for learning by sounds, sight reading for learning by vision, and writing drills for learning by motor means.

Differences in children's reactions suggest not only how they will learn best at school, but also how they can get the most from homework assignments. Parents should not make any blanket rules for study without first considering their suitability for the particular child. As an example, what rule should be made about studying with the radio or phonograph on? Some children are distracted by noises, and the radio or phonograph should never be on when they are studying. On the other hand, there *are* others who concentrate better when soft music seals out other distractions. Still other children don't even *hear* the music, and it makes no difference whether it is on or not.

Not all children can excel, or even should try to excel, in school. Not all children, even under the best auspices, will want to climb to the top of the educational ladder. But all normally intelligent ones— adaptable, nonadaptable, active, leisurely, persistent, distractible, quiet, or intense—can be interested in learning. Success in school for any child will depend in large measure on the development of his positive interest, in addition to his I.Q. level. It is our experience that recognizing a child's style of learning and encouraging him to learn in the way that is most effective for him helps prevent the frustration, discouragement, and loss of interest that so often initiates or intensifies school problems.

19 THE WORKING MOTHER: NOT GUILTY!

A young woman doctor was about to begin her psychiatric training in a leading Midwestern hospital. When the director of the psychiatric service heard that she was going to have a baby shortly before she began her training, he urged her strongly to stay home with her baby and postpone her hospital work. He did not think a woman who would risk the emotional health of her own child in order to get her training would make a good psychiatrist.

Another young woman, a psychologist, told her husband happily that she had found the perfect job. Her hours would match those of her three-and-a-half-year-old son's nursery-school day, and she would also be able to stay home with him whenever he was sick or on vacation. Her husband, a psychoanalyst, insisted that she turn down the job. He said that the child would be emotionally damaged by her working, even if she was always home when the youngster was. He maintained that simply having an outside interest would divert concern and attention that their son needed.

These incidents both occurred within the past few years, not fifty years ago. The opinions of the two psychiatrists may appear extreme. The truth is, however, that a large and influential professional group still believes that mother's place is in the home. A prominent psychoanalyst writes: [1] "My own experience with working mothers indicates once again that the predominant emotion they feel is guilt. I have no choice but to believe this guilt is the price exacted for maternal neglect in the interests of self-enhancement."

He then offers a solution for women who want to work which will prevent this "maternal neglect": "Marry young, have your children between eighteen and twenty-four, spend the next fourteen years giving them effective care, and then enter on a career." How a mother is to deal with the difficulties, and even the impossibility, of starting a career when she is almost forty is not mentioned. And what should the millions of mothers who *have* to work to support their children do: Stay home living on relief or work and endanger the children's well-being?

The assertion by many psychiatrists and psychologists that the working mother hurts her children causes a mixture of anxiety, guilt, and resentment in large numbers of women. Many of our professional consultations over the years have centered on this problem. Mothers come for advice and help because they are caught between the desire to have a job and the fear of what it will do to their children. Some are working and feel selfish and unnatural for doing it. They may then drive themselves to excesses of devotion to their children to atone for their sins. Other mothers who want to work don't, and then feel frustrated and resent the children who "keep them from working." Resentment leads to guilt. This mixture of frustration, guilt, and resentment is hardly beneficial to mother or child.

We cannot be sure how many of the seven and a half million working mothers in this country with children under twelve are disturbed by conflict and guilt over working. But whether disturbed or not, whether working by choice or necessity, this same question is of vital concern to all of them and to their families: Does a mother hurt her child by working outside the home?

A century of struggle for women's rights has counted as one of its great achievements the increasing acceptance of women into all types of jobs and professions. Has this struggle been wrong because it has led millions of mothers to work outside the home? Should these mothers give up their jobs and learn to live with whatever frustration this brings them?

What is the evidence for these oft-repeated assertions that the working mother may be "neglecting" her child? As in a number of other parent-child issues it turns out that the "evidence" is primarily theory and not fact. The theory asserts that a child's healthy psychological development requires a *continuous* relationship with a loving, nurturing mother from birth to adolescence. Various reasons are offered. Most influential has been the psychoanalytic concept that the child's healthy progress through predetermined stages of presumed instinctual development depends most of all on the continual contact with a nurturing mother.

Reinforcing these assertions that the good mother is the one committed exclusively to child nurture are the Freudian ideas that the woman who works is "denying her femininity" and "striving for masculinity." That Freud held to such concepts might be explained as a reflection of the Victorian prejudices and Central European stereotypes of his day. But the same ideas are found in some recent psychoanalytic writings. Typical of this continued trend is the volume *The Psychology of Women* by a prominent analyst, Dr. Helene Deutsch. Written in 1944, this book is still recommended in various current psychiatric writings as an authoritative statement of the orthodox Freudian position. In this volume Dr. Deutsch maintains that there are "three essential traits of femininity—narcissism, passivity and masochism"; that these are fixed, unchangeable characteristics; and that "the fundamental identities 'feminine-passive' and 'masculine-active' asserted themselves in all known cultures and races." She labels the progress made by women in entering fields of work hitherto closed to them as an "invasion of the masculine professions" through which "the masculinization of women was unmistakably expressed." She suggests that women give up work in the outside world and return to the home, "to the basically conservative because always dominant feminine experience."

It can be stated categorically that these Freudian formulations on the nature of femininity are not supported by any of the serious research studies in anthropology, psychology, or clinical psychiatry.

The "evidence" offered to buttress the claim that the child whose mother is not continuously at home will suffer deprivation comes primarily from two sources: 1) psychiatric case material, and 2) studies of children separated from their mothers during their early years.

Innumerable case studies of children and adults with psychiatric problems have indicated that many of these individuals suffered from maternal mishandling and neglect in childhood. There is no doubt that a bad mother will have an unhealthy influence on her child's development. But the *quality* of motherhood should not be confused with *quantity*. The fact that good mothering is important does not mean that it has to be administered twenty-four hours a day every day. The question at issue is whether a *good* mother who works can still give her child adequate nurturing and love in the hours she spends at home with him.

A number of studies in the thirties and forties reported that children who had been completely separated from their mothers in infancy showed serious defects in personality and intellectual development. These abnormalities were attributed to the absence of the mother. It was then assumed that any child separated from his mother even for short intervals would suffer in his development.[2]

Recently, however, a number of child-development research workers have questioned whether the link these early studies made between separation and abnormal development was quite as clear and inevitable as it seemed. They have pointed out that the study children had so many serious problems in early life—emotionally ill parents, poverty, racial discrimination, serious illness, mental retardation, family conflict—that it was unsound to trace the blame for faulty development to any single cause. They also noted that when one considered the sterile, impersonal, and often grossly inadequate care given the children in the institutions and in the succession of foster-homes in which many of them grew up, one could not fairly lay their troubles to the fact of separation itself.[3]

Finally, a number of reports began to appear of children separated from their mothers and brought up in institutions who *did not* develop the psychological abnormalities described in the earlier studies.[4]

The effects of separation from the mother where the children are normal and receive good substitute care have also been investigated. Of special interest is a recent follow-up study of twenty young adults in London who as children had been evacuated from their families during the wartime blitz of London and settled in nurseries around the countryside for periods ranging from one to five years. Their mothers remained in the city and visited their children when they could. As young adults most of these twenty individuals are now functioning normally. Only 25 per cent (five cases) show any significant degree of abnormal behavior, but almost without exception this group has grown up in disturbed families after their return home. All in all, there is no evidence to support the idea that separation from the mother as such had any serious effects on the development of the group studied.[5]

The effect of partial separation of children from working mothers has also been studied in agricultural communities in Israel, the *kibbutzim*. In these communities most mothers work, and their young children are brought up in group nurseries. The parents visit daily, but the children are cared for by competent nursery workers. Children brought up in this fashion have been evaluated by teams of psychologists and no significant personality defects found.[6]

Two recent professional articles have reviewed and summarized the large number of studies of the working mother reported in recent years. One review concludes that "the findings from existing research concerning the working mother . . . supply little support to the viewers-with-alarm." [7] The other author comments that "it looks as if the fact of the mother being employed or staying at home is not such an important factor in determining the behavior of the child as we have been led to think." [8] There is also no evidence that the working mother is less maternal, but several studies indicate that she often has anxiety and guilt over working.[9] This guilt is not surprising, considering how often she is reproached for "neglecting" her children.

Our own research study yields no evidence that children suffer when their mothers work. Eight of the mothers went back to full-time work when their children were two to three months old. The only child who showed any adverse reaction was one whose responses, from the beginning, had been irregular, nonadaptive, intense, and predominantly negative—the temperamental characteristics of a difficult child. The mother's schedule at home and the time spent with the child after she returned to work were irregular and inconsistent. This, rather than the fact of working, appears to be responsible for the youngster's maladjustment. Even this child finally adapted after his mother's schedule became regular and consistent.

Thirty-two other mothers in our study went back to part-time work when their children were anywhere between three months and five years of age. We have not been able to detect any significant emotional differences in their children as compared to the others in the study.

There has also been no evidence that the working mothers in our study are less maternal or less feminine than the other mothers.

To summarize, the evidence from existing research studies is overwhelmingly in favor of the verdict "Not guilty." The fact that a woman works need not interfere with her children's development.

The quality of parent-child relationship is more important than the amount of time involved. When a mother and child get along well, the child will usually get along equally well if the mother works, provided that he is well cared for in her absence.

If the mother and child don't get along well and the mother goes to work, they may go right on disagreeing at home. Stopping work, however, won't mend things.

Sometimes a mother-child relationship may even improve when the mother goes to work. A woman who chafes at the unalleviated round of diapers, cooking, housework, and the absence of adult stimulation may experience a resurgence of motherly love after her return to work. She may find her patience restored, her reactions calmer, and her responses wiser. Her children will share the benefits of the greater relaxation and cheerfulness.

There are times when a mother's place is at home and no one else can do quite as well. The youngster who is easily upset when his mother and he are separated even briefly would suffer if she picked this time to start a job or even go away for a trip. The child's problem of dependency should be solved first.

There are many other occasions when mothers of little children are very much needed: at the start of nursery school, for birthday parties, when children are going to or returning from the hospital, at important school events, during acute illness, at PTA and class meetings, when there is an accident or death, etc.

The mother who has to work to support her child and herself should not be placed in the terrible predicament of having to choose between her job and her child's welfare. There should be a good community-supported day nursery or after-school center available to look after her youngster while she is working. And if her child is ill or otherwise needs her at home, her job should not be jeopardized.

While we would hope that mothers will be relieved of feeling guilty about working, we would certainly hate to see them come to feel guilty or less intelligent, attractive, or fulfilled about wanting to stay home. A working-class mother who could only find dull factory jobs usually does not want to work unless she has to help support the family. There are also many middle-class women whose interests and inclination lead them to devote their time, energy, and talents to family and community. Downgrading this choice would seem to be as destructive of their individuality as the pressure to keep women home has been in the past.

Any stereotyped formula about the working mother is inaccurate and harmful. Providing economic circumstances make it possible, a young mother should be free to stay home or combine home and career. Either choice should be possible without guilt about hypothetical damage to the children.

20 THE "LATE BLOOMER"

Parents have always attached a great deal of importance to when a child begins to stand, walk, and talk. It is still a common belief that precocity in these developmental achievements is a sign of superior intelligence. Hence, when a child fails to stand up, walk, or speak at precisely the prescribed age, parents begin to worry. They may try to relax by reminding themselves that cousin Harry, who didn't speak a word until he was three, graduated from college as a member of Phi Beta Kappa and was president of the debating team. But such reminders are not always effective in stilling their fears. The belief continues to prevail that most children who are slow at walking and talking will also be retarded intellectually.

It is true that most of the mentally retarded are slow in all areas of development, and many children who walk and talk at phenomenally early ages grow up to function at very superior intellectual levels. However, a direct relationship between the age of walking and talking and later intellectual level exists for only a small minority of youngsters. One child who walks at ten months and says his first word at nine months may become a mathematical wizard. Another such "infant prodigy" may turn out to be average intellectually. A third child who didn't take a step or say a word until his second birthday may develop as remarkable intellectual powers as an early starter. There is very little evidence that anything parents do will significantly accelerate or slow up the child's own rate of development.

A delay in walking usually is only briefly worrisome to parents, because the delay is short unless some definite abnormality is present. Practically all normal children begin to walk by eighteen months, and even the slow starters will be trotting around like any other child by the time they are two.

If a child does not walk at all by eighteen months, it is time to consult a specialist. A number of orthopedic or neurological conditions, having nothing to do with intellectual functioning, may be responsible, such as congenital hip dislocation, cerebral palsy, or muscular disease.

A language delay may last longer and therefore be more worrisome. The normal child who has not said his first word at twelve months may take another year or sometimes even two to begin talking. If a child is still not talking at all by two years, a consultation with a specialist recommended by the child's pediatrician is indicated to determine whether the speech lag indicates some special disturbance in development.

The specialist can estimate the nontalking child's general level of mental development by a number of simple tests. If the child is up to age level, parents can be reassured that he is not retarded and that the language problem is a specific developmental delay that will gradually disappear after he begins to talk.

Even when testing shows his general behavior to be below normal level, the delayed talker may not necessarily be mentally retarded. The child may be showing the consequences of parental anxiety and overprotectiveness. Some parents try to shield a child from frustration by jumping in and doing things for him before he has a chance to try for himself. When this happens to the very adaptable baby who is neither very persistent nor very intense, he will simply let the parent take over and will not learn to do things for himself.

The assertive, persistent child, on the other hand, will struggle against his parents' interference and will keep trying to master new activities and tasks on his own. His development is therefore less likely to be affected by overprotective parents.

Like the late walkers, normal children who are slow to talk usually catch up in time, with some taking longer than others to achieve a speech level normal for their years. There are a few late talkers, however, who are very slow in making up for their slow start. Despite good intelligence and normal psychological development, they may lag behind not only in speech but also in learning to read and write. Professional evaluation and guidance can help overcome the learning problems this kind of developmental lag creates.

In a small number of cases marked delay in talking may be a sign of brain damage or serious mental illness. In such children there are other accompanying signs, such as bizarre behavior of various kinds, which will indicate that the child is not developing normally. Special professional help is necessary for such children. (See Chapter 22.)

Late walking rarely leaves any significant psychological consequences. At most, parents and older brothers and sisters may have to carry the child around a few months longer than usual. But delay in speech development attracts more attention and may cause more trouble. The late talker must cope with the frustration of not being able to communicate his thoughts and wishes. Though mentally and physically as capable as his peers, he is cut off from them to some extent by not being able to express himself.

In addition, he may be the subject of derogatory comments from people who assume that, because he can't speak, he can't understand, or from others who interpret his failure to respond as bad manners. Other children, too, may make fun of the child who doesn't talk.

Late talkers differ in their reaction to frustration and ridicule. The child who adapts easily and who has predominantly mild and positive reactions may not be badly upset by criticism and teasing. One very bright little girl in our study whose speech development was greatly delayed remained cheerful and gregarious through nursery school and kindergarten, in spite of her difficulty in making herself understood by teacher and classmates. Because of this positive adaptability, her social relations with adults and other children developed normally even through her years of slow language development.

Parents cannot shield the intense nontalker with predominant negative mood reactions from frustrating experiences. Overprotection is hard to avoid, but it is *not* helpful. Restricting the child's activities and experiences to save him from frustration only adds social retardation to the difficulties created by his speech lag. Nor does it help for the parent to rush in and talk *for* him when the youngster gives up in tears or runs away. This may only encourage his tendency to have tantrums or retreat whenever he can't make himself understood.

While warning against overprotection, we are not recommending a Spartan attitude for its own sake. It is certainly not wise for parents to refuse a child's wishes until he puts them into words. This does not help the child's language development. On the contrary, it may add an emotional block to his speech problem.

What are the positive ways to help? The slow talker appreciates and benefits from all kinds of stimulating experiences. He needs more, not fewer, adventures than other children do, even if his ability to show what he's learned is temporarily limited. He also needs whatever protection parents can give him from the derogatory remarks of insensitive adults. Such comments can be countered with a clear statement that the child is intelligent and understands everything people say, even though he hasn't begun to talk. Sometimes the remarks can be prevented if parents can explain a child's speech delay to strangers before he meets them.

Fortunately, almost all normal children with speech lag leave their problems and frustrations behind them after they begin to talk. A few may need speech therapy to help them overcome habits of poor pronunciation. A small number need some help to get over the behavior problems they developed from their frustrating early years. But most go on in their later development with no significant residue from this early period of stress.

Children with speech delay may show signs later of being slow in the area of written language development, that is, in reading. Such reading difficulties should be attended to early. With appropriate remedial-reading instruction the problem can often be successfully overcome so that the child is able to read at the normal level before his school work becomes too demanding.

Another type of developmental lag is in general muscular coordination. Children with this problem walk clumsily and seem generally awkward, whether at play or dresssing and feeding themselves. Usually the delay is temporary. The badly coordinated toddler most often finally becomes average, and sometimes even better than average, in motor skills. Sometimes, however, the poor coordination is more extensive and for that reason less likely to be outgrown. In such cases professional consultation is necessary to determine whether therapy should be started to improve muscular functioning.

The child who is poorly coordinated, like the youngster who talks late, will inevitably miss out on some of the normal give-and-take with his age mates. Being a bad runner and climber, or a slow-poke, or unable to keep up with the rest of the tricycle-racing crowd may be frustrating. It may also make a child the butt of the group.

Here, too, as with other developmental lags, the degree of frustration depends a great deal on the child's temperamental characteristics. The easily adaptable, mild, and predominantly positive youngster will usually be much less distressed than his opposite number.

Parents can help minimize the problem by treating the poorly coordinated youngster as much as possible like a normal child. He will need more experience trying his muscles, rather than less. He should never be kept from trying simply for fear he will be frustrated in his attempt. He can be stimulated by being helped to succeed when he does try, and by being encouraged to practice with patient assistance. The kind of help the parent should give also depends on whether the child is temperamentally persistent or nonpersistent. The persistent youngster usually doesn't need much encouragement to practice; he will do it on his own. He may, however, need assistance when the task is too hard for him. Otherwise his unsuccessful persistence may lead to frustration. The nonpersistent child, on the other hand, may need encouragement and even urging to keep him from giving up too quickly.

In general, the issues are similar with any developmental lag. First, the child should be checked for any abnormality of physical or mental development which sometimes can cause such lags. If no such abnormality exists, the child's development can be expected to catch up eventually. Until then he may show varying degrees of stress and frustration, depending on his temperamental characteristics. Parents can help in many ways. They can assist the easily frustrated child by making the difficult situations a little easier for him. They can encourage the nonpersistent child to try more when indicated. They can explain the problem to strangers. When necessary, they can get professional advice about the best way to help their child.

In most cases late starters make up for lost time eventually and, if helped properly by parents and others, end up none the worse for lagging behind initially.

21 THE HANDICAPPED CHILD

Almost one child in twenty is born with a congenital defect sufficiently serious for him to require special care and training. The
mentally retarded group is the largest, comprising 2.3 per cent
of all births. There are also children who are mentally or physically handicapped by brain injury without retardation. Others are
born blind or deaf. Heart abnormalities limit the activity and
threaten the health of large numbers, and other less familiar defects handicap the lives of thousands of additional children. Because of accidents or illness in very early life many more children
become handicapped, physically or mentally.

The parents' goal for the handicapped child is of course the
same as it would be for any child—to help him develop so that he
will make the most of himself and get the best out of life. When
the child's prospects are seriously restricted, this goal necessarily
becomes a much more difficult undertaking.

The level of functioning a handicapped child can achieve in life
depends on many factors: the nature and severity of the defect, the
effectiveness of medical treatment and rehabilitation procedures,
the approach of the parents, the temperamental characteristics of
the child, the nature of the family and the neighborhood, and the
special facilities available in the community.

It goes without saying that the child should have the benefit of
everything that medical science can offer. Any and all procedures
that can correct or improve his handicap or train him to minimize the crippling effects of his defect should be the first order of
business for him at all times. Parents can get advice and guidance

in these directions from a number of excellent agencies and associations.[1]

Unfortunately, some parents feel so overwhelmed and helpless after the birth of a defective child that they are unable to accept the truth about his limitations. Such parents may have to be urged to seek out the special medical centers and institutions that can help their child and ease their own responsibilities.

Parent responsibilities with a handicapped child are demanding and complex. The child needs parents who can listen to instruction from specialists and follow it explicitly. Parents must not overprotect the child from demands that he is capable of meeting, must withstand the impulse to help too soon, and patiently wait for the child to succeed through many failures and disappointments. The handicapped child also needs to be shielded from situations that he cannot cope with. Yet the parents must have time, in addition, to devote to the other children in the family.

A parent who faces the problems realistically, gets the necessary professional help and guidance, and acts accordingly will often be amazed at how much can be accomplished. The retarded child who learns to play with other children, the youngster with muscular defects who begins to travel alone, the deaf child who masters speech and lip reading—all should give satisfaction to parents by their achievements in moving into the mainstream of life. Parents who mobilize their energies constructively for a handicapped child help not only the child, but also the rest of the family and themselves. This is true not only for the parent as an individual with his own child, but also for parents functioning in groups. The remarkable spontaneous development of parent groups organized for specific defects and illnesses—mental retardation, cerebral palsy, muscular dystrophy, cystic fibrosis, and so on—attests to the value and importance of healthy parent activity for handicapped youngsters.

Many parents lose their bearings in helping their handicapped child because of guilt feelings. Guilt can mushroom for different reasons. It is normal enough for a mother's first words after giving birth to be "Is he all right?" But if she bears a child who is not "perfect" and feels, almost like women in primitive times, that she is in some mysterious way to blame, she will be burdened with guilt feelings. If the parents are frightened of the problems of caring for the child and long to be spared the responsibilities ahead, they may become guilty for having such thoughts. If they have read certain popular articles or watched special TV programs, they may get the impression that they should have exactly the same feeling for their retarded child as they have for their normal children. Guilt may develop when they find they haven't the same interest and enthusiasm for the retarded youngster's slow progress and meager achievements. Actually, to expect the parent to respond the same way no matter what his child is like is unrealistic and unreasonable.

Shame can also disorient the parent's approach. Shame, in turn, often leads to guilt at being ashamed. Some handicaps in children are more socially acceptable than others. Most physical defects, like blindness, deafness, heart disorder, or paralysis, are viewed objectively as tragedies that are nobody's fault. Parents of children with such handicaps know that they and their youngster are regarded with sympathy. Most people will be glad to help them if they can. This makes it much easier for the parents to have sympathy, compassion, and concern for their child, uncontaminated by shame or resentment.

Unfortunately, even in this enlightened day, other handicaps are sometimes viewed differently. Severe obesity in a child all too frequently makes him an object of ridicule. Mentally retarded children are often still the butt of jokes by other children and teased by some adults as well. Not only does this make it hard for the parents to maintain their own positive feelings toward the child, but the child can be badly damaged psychologically by such social disapproval.

Sometimes parents will expiate their shame and guilt by lavishing excessive devotion on the handicapped child. This is bad for the youngster, who may become so sheltered that his chance of becoming a relatively independent individual is forfeited. It is bad for the other children in the family, who may get so little attention from the parents that their full emotional or intellectual development may be impaired.

Guilt feelings may paralyze the parents' ability to make important decisions for the child's future. This can happen, for example, when a severely retarded child requires care in an institution. The pediatrician and other specialists they have consulted may have told the parents that the child would do better in a center where the best diagnosticians, the most experienced therapists, and the best equipment are available. The parents may know that this will also be much better for the welfare of the rest of the family, but they may then be bedeviled by the guilty feeling that they want the child to be cared for in an institution in order to be rid of him. If they have also heard that the mentally retarded child needs his parents' love even more than normal children, they may be so tormented that they keep putting off the inevitable decision.[2]

The best antidote for guilt feelings or shame is for the parent to get busy helping the child. Working with other parents in one of the voluntary oganizations for handicapped children also is beneficial. Such constructive activity often does wonders in diminishing and even eliminating unhealthy feelings. If this does not work, discussions with a qualified counselor may be desirable.

Appreciation of the role that affection and acceptance play in the life of any child has prompted some overoptimistic statements about what love can do for the mentally retarded. Being part of an affectionate family can certainly improve the emotional health and influence the behavior of the mentally handicapped child. But it is not magic. Some problems cannot be loved away. Love cannot make companions in the neighborhood who will enjoy playing with a child who does not understand or respond appropriately. Love cannot make the retarded child feel wanted and successful when children tease or run away. In addition to love, the retarded child needs patient, calm, and persistent teachers, both in the family and in special schools, so that he can develop his full potential. Only this can give him the sense of self-confidence that comes from progressive mastery and achievement.

Success in handling the retarded child will depend as much on his individual temperament as it will on his parents' approach, as is the case with the development of normal children.

An easily adaptable, predominantly mild and positive child who is retarded may be slow to understand and follow directions or rules for a game, but if he is gentle, pleasant, and reasonably quiet, other children will often accept him and even take care of him and look after his interests. This kind of child can usually learn necessary social habit patterns without too much difficulty. He can learn to obey the rules. He can be toilet trained. He can learn to feed and dress himself when he reaches the intellectual age corresponding to the actual age at which normal children can do such things.

The intense, highly active, slowly adaptable, and negative child will have different life experiences, even if his retardation is mild. He will quickly wear out his welcome with other children because of the combination of his slowness in understanding, his impulsiveness, and his loud tantrums. They will try to keep him out of their games because they know he will spoil everything. This kind of retarded child more frequently needs to be put in a special school than does the easy, amiable one. Only such a school may be able to teach him the minimum necessary rules for playing and living with other children or with grownups.

Temperamental characteristics may also be important influences in the development of other kinds of handicapped children. This is illustrated by the stories of three brain-injured children in our study.

One child had a minor muscular weakness and poor coordination. Although he had superior intelligence, he didn't say a word until he was four years old. When he did speak, he needed speech therapy for several years to correct his babyish pronunciation. He was an easily adaptable, mild, and positive child, whose amiability and pleasantness made the parents' role during the first years much easier. They were advised that they could demand reasonable behavior from him and should avoid babying him. He responded well, and his behavior developed normally.

He was teased by both adults and children, first when he did not talk, and later when he talked baby talk. But his parents didn't react very much, except to assure him repeatedly and casually that he would catch up and not to worry. He remained cheerful in spite of teasing and was accepted as a playmate by almost all the children in the playground and school. His parents saw to it that he drilled on his corrective speech work so that he would catch up faster. Now, at eight, his speech and coordination are approaching normal.

The second youngster had more marked muscular weakness and

was also mildly retarded intellectually. Like the first child, he was an easy child temperamentally. His care and training did not create any family problems. He has grown up to be a mild-mannered, pleasant little boy who has played easily with normal children. His parents have had professional guidance, and he is developing better than his handicaps might originally have suggested.

The third child with brain damage had the temperamental characteristics of the difficult child. Though not retarded intellectually, she showed irregularity, nonadaptability, intensity, and negative mood reactions, which, combined with the brain damage, created problems that were increasingly difficult to handle. It was hard to train her for even the simplest routines. She shrieked loudly and long with any upset. When she began to walk, her sudden movements and awkward coordination caused frequent accidents. Her irregular sleeping habits and persistent demands for attention made the bedtime ritual drag out longer and longer. By the time she was three, it could take all evening to get her to sleep. She had to be tucked in and retucked in, in a special way; she requested certain songs in a certain order, a particular number of kisses and nonsense phrases in ritual fashion, and went into hysterics at any slip-up.

Calm, imperturbable parents with unlimited time and energy might have gradually established some controls. But this child's father and mother had two other children who also required time and attention. It was clear that the health and welfare of all concerned would be better served if the child went to a special residential school.

The care of a handicapped child at home depends first of all on the severity of the handicap. In some cases where the handicap, physical or mental, is very serious, it may be impossible to care for the child at home. Where the handicap is mild, the care of the child at home may be relatively easy. It is in the large in-between group that a choice has to be made.

How does one decide? By weighing as dispassionately as possible the needs of the child and the needs of the rest of the family, and then making a judgment about how everyone can be served best.

Sometimes older children can be very helpful in sharing some of the responsibility for a handicapped brother or sister. If their own development is not being threatened by his presence, they may be able to establish mutual warmth and affection with the less fortunate family member. The experience of adapting to a brother or sister who needs special care and attention and who reciprocates with steadfast devotion and loyalty can have immeasurable value for normal children.

The nature of the neighborhood and community is also important. The retarded or otherwise handicapped child who can find accepting and acceptable playmates in the neighborhood has a better chance of making it at home. Special day schools, play groups, helpful professional agencies, and parent groups can be of great value if they exist in the community. Many communities have them in abundance. Others, unfortunately, have none.

Parents should investigate the institutional care available for the child and then compare the advantages of family life with the special benefits of residential care. The first question may be: Can the home and the community supply the kind of treatment and training that the child's doctor feels will develop the maximum degree of independent fuctioning? Or will the child require equipment and specialized knowledge that only a residential center and a highly trained staff can give? Some handicapped children may need institutional care for limited periods of time to achieve specific training goals. The child can then return home with his level of functioning substantially higher than before.

Parents of handicapped children are often reassured when they see for themselves the success that specialized treatment centers and schools can have in training severely handicapped children to achieve proficient handling of their environment. These institutions can persevere in moving their pupils steadily toward greater independence and self-sufficiency in a way that is often not possible at home. They also can frequently supply congenial companions and playmates that a child's home neighborhood cannot.

One of us remembers a festival at a children's orthopedic convalescent hospital. A large group of children were playing a circle game. There were children in braces and wheelchairs, and one with two artificial legs. In the course of the game, this last child slipped and fell. It was interesting that the other children, the teachers, *and* the child himself appeared quite unconcerned. The game waited while he slowly and laboriously picked himself up again. Then the game went on as before.

Whether at home or in a special treatment center, the goal for the handicapped child is to protect him when necessary, while teaching him to function independently as much as possible. The more he learns to get along on his own, the healthier will be his emotional development and the more normal will be the life he can lead. The outcome for each child will depend on the interplay of the many influences we have discussed above. But in each case the parents' willingness to take a constructive approach, and to use professional services and community resources, offers the handicapped child an opportunity to develop fully his own resources.

22 HOW TO SPOT TROUBLE

Parents naturally become concerned when their child behaves in a way that doesn't seem normal. On the other hand, most parents realize that no child will behave perfectly at all times. How can a parent know when a problem is really a PROBLEM? When should a child's behavior be of sufficient concern to seek professional advice?

Unfortunately, there are no explicit general signs of mental ill health. There are no fevers as in infection, no spots as in measles, nor swellings as in mumps. Furthermore, in the child's early years development proceeds so rapidly and behavior changes so quickly that it is especially difficult to assess deviations from the normal and pinpoint the beginnings of trouble.

Sometimes difficult behavior is only an exaggeration of a normal developmental phase. This could be called the psychological equivalent of growing pains. Two-year-old Joey learns the word "no" and drives his mother frantic. Three-year-old Sally begins to tease and her older sister explodes with anger. Four-year-old David insists that his dinner seat and knife and fork be set exactly the same each evening and keeps the whole family standing and fuming while adjustments of a half-inch are made. Dr. Arnold Gesell's description of these developmental phases has helped innumerable parents to wait until their children "grew out of it."

Sometimes deviant behavior reflects temporary adjustment difficulties. Sammy, aged three, starts off at nursery school as happy as can be, only to turn right around three weeks later and cling to his mother like a baby at the classroom door. It turns out that the other boys' roughhouse play has frightened him. Four-year-old Jimmy, always an amicable child until the next baby was born, now has a tantrum every time his daddy goes near the new baby's crib. Allen, aged five, has just suffered the death of his beloved grandmother. His kindergarten teacher reports that he has begun to stutter. Six-year-old Ruthy, who always adjusts slowly to new situations, begins to wet her bed when the family moves from a house in the country to an apartment in the city.

These are typical developmental and adjustment problems that crop up in most children. Some children have a few, others have many. In almost all cases they come and go quickly, either because the problems are self-limited in time, like a cold, or because the parents know how to handle them and do so, almost without thinking. But if the behavior grows worse with time instead of better, professional help is indicated.

Problems can develop if parents expect a child to act like some dream-child of their imagination instead of being *himself*. For example, a few years ago a mother consulted us about her five-year-old son. She was afraid he was schizophrenic because he was very quiet and withdrawn. He wouldn't play baseball or skate with the other children and was even reluctant to go outdoors.

The boy looked like a handsome, solemn, quiet, hesitant youngster. We invited him into the playroom to see how he would adapt to a new situation and a new person, and how he would play.

For a few minutes he sat quietly, looking around at everything in the room. Then he walked over to the blocks, carefully examined each size and shape, and then began to play, eventually bringing in dolls, cars, and so on. When he wanted to know what some unfamiliar object was or how to use it, he asked us without hesitating. Gradually he began to tell us what he played with at home and what he liked about the toys that were new to him.

There was nothing at all the matter with the youngster. He was just not the ideal boy his mother had anticipated. She was a vigorous, active woman who had been a tomboy and couldn't wait to live vicariously a *real* boy's life, through her son. In her efforts to make him conform to her ideal, she had pressured him to become a bubbling, gregarious athlete. He had resisted, not by violent protests, but in his characteristic fashion by quiet retreat. It is possible that this retreat might eventually have made him a seriously withdrawn child.

The mother was relieved to know that her boy was not sick, but she was still disappointed that he was not quite the boy she had ordered. However, when she saw that trying to make him what he was not might keep him from being *anyone,* she controlled her disappointment and began to let him be himself.

With the pressure off, this little boy did what he would have done in the first place if he could have operated in his own way. His natural curiosity about what was going on outside led him right out the front door. At first, there was plenty to interest him in the soil, in the bushes and flowers, and in bird and insect life. When other children came, he slowly found his role in the group. He never became a star athlete, but he liked to be in the games, and he was invariably called upon to settle disputes, make decisions, umpire close plays.

Another mother, a woman who spent the spare moments she could snatch between household chores and caring for her children in reading or listening to records, consulted us because her son was so wild she thought he was ill. She, too, was making a judgment based on what she thought children should be rather than on what her child *was*.

After we reviewed the child's history with her, it became clear that he was very active, curious, and distractible. His mother had tried to turn him into her ideal, a studious child who could play quietly for long periods by himself. The more she tried, the "wilder" he became, literally running around in circles making a lot of noise.

When the mother recognized that her youngster could still be normal even if he didn't fit her stereotype, she began to handle him differently. His noisy activities were no longer inhibited as long as he abided by simple rules that were set up for his safety and for the comfort of the rest of the family. His "wildness" subsided, though he never became the gentle, studious boy his mother had dreamed of.

It was good that these mothers came for professional advice. A parent cannot always judge accurately if a child who behaves differently from the stereotype of the normal is doing what is normal for himself or is really developing a problem. Even if no problem is present, parents can often use guidance in the best ways of helping a child whose temperament is difficult for them to accept constructively.

Slowness in physical or language development can also become a matter of concern (see Chapters 20 and 21). In the rare cases when serious mental illness occurs in childhood, parents can easily recognize that something is very wrong because of the child's bizarre behavior and speech. Specialized psychiatric management of such a child is always necessary.

Less severe behavior problems often look like an exaggerated form of the child's normal behavior or appear as arrested development in one area or several. Children under eight—*almost without exception*—go through periods when they may have any or all of the following symptoms in varying degrees of intensity.

1. *Sleep problems*

Some children wake up most nights and cry. Others climb out of bed, wander around the house, or want to get into their parents' bed. Most children, like grownups, will have an occasional bad dream. Some children have more frightening and more frequent ones. They may involve wild animals, monsters, being lost in a forest, etc.

2. *Fears*

A child may insist on crossing to the other side of the street every time he sees a dog, he may be afraid to go outside for fear of meeting a cat, he may refuse to enter a room containing a sculptured figure, or he may run and hide every time the vacuum cleaner is turned on. He may be afraid of school and vomit almost every morning before setting out.

3. *Excessive timidity*

A three-year-old might scream when pushed in a swing or set on a slide. Another child might seem too retiring, letting himself be pushed out of the line at the drinking fountain until his mother comes to get him a place. He might also seem very timid playing with other children, giving up his toys too easily and then looking bereft and helpless, instead of finding something else to do or someone else to play with.

4. *Play problems*

Some children at three or four remain on the side lines in nursery school even after they have been with the group for months, and can join in some group activity only when the teacher takes great pains to involve them.

Other children seem to be much *too* dependent on company, though it doesn't matter much to them who the companions are. The child doesn't really involve them in his play. They are used more or less like window dressing or space fillers.

5. *General dissatisfaction*

Nothing pleases. Nothing turns out right. Neither solicitude and indulgence, more rest, more attention from parents, nor firmer, more consistent discipline seem to change the child's general attitude of sadness and discontent.

6. *Extreme negativism*

Instead of being firm about some things he doesn't like, as most children are, the extreme negativist will seem to be saying "no" on principle, and saying it much more emphatically than is necessary or appropriate. Rather than responding with a "no" and adding a few whines or tears to make a point, he may throw repeated tantrums. He seems impelled to almost frenetic protest against anything anyone wants him to do, have, or be, and he is similarly resistant to stopping anything he wants to do or giving up anything he has.

7. *Clinging*

A three-year-old may cling to his mother's side during the week or more she stays at nursery school, then cling to the teacher in the same way after his mother stops coming; a child may sit beside her mother in the park every day, getting up only when her mother takes her to the swing or sits with her in the sandbox helping her shovel.

8. *Moving backwards*

While children's general growth is forward toward more physical, intellectual, and emotional proficiency, some show setbacks. The thumb-sucker appears to stop and then begins again; the trained child suddenly relapses; the baby who sleeps through the night starts waking and screaming at 2 A.M.; the child who has gone quite willingly to nursery school doesn't want to go at all five months later.

These behavior problems may come and go even with normal children. How, then, do parents know when such problems signal a need for more expert attention than they can give?

Parents might ask: *"Is this like him?"* Unexpected, unusual reactions to situations—behavior that appears quite out of character for the child—are more cause for concern than a slightly pronounced version of the child's natural behavior. For example, clinging behavior in a little boy who has always been outgoing and positive in his reactions to people and places would be more worrisome than the same behavior in a more hesitant, slowly adapting child of the same age.

"Is there a reason?" One expects children, and adults, too, to show some effects of an external strain, stress, or shock. If a child has lost a friend or relative, or had an accident or a major scare of any kind, if he has had to cope with an unusual number of changes in routine and environment, parents should expect some kind of reaction, varying in degree and kind according to the individual temperament of the child. If the manifestations are mild and disappear quickly, they can be considered a normal response to acute stress. If there is an unusually long, adverse reaction to a frightening experience or to unusual temporary stress or strain, this might very well deserve professional exploration. It may be dis-

covered that a behavior problem was developing unnoticed before the frightening experience. The acute stress had then served to heighten the disturbance and crystallize its symptoms. For example, a five-year-old boy experienced the sudden death of his grandfather. He developed nightmares and fears of growing up and dying. When, in the next few months, the fears did not diminish but rather grew worse, the problem was investigated. It turned out that he had been showing mild fears and occasional nightmares even before his grandfather's death. He had an intellectually superior older sister who was openly favored by the parents, and he was afraid that when he grew up and went to school he could never live up to his sister's performance. His reaction to his grandfather's death served to reinforce and intensify the fears which were already present.

"Is it spreading?" What requires investigation is deviant behavior that is not simply an isolated affair—such as one fear or a single area of clinging—but a number of related or even unrelated kinds of troubling reactions that don't seem to be getting better, but may even be spreading and involving more and more of the child's daily routines.

One boy, four-year-old Kenny, developed a fear of dogs after a large dog unexpectedly jumped on him and cut his lip. For several months after this event he asked repeatedly and anxiously, "Is there a dog?" "Will they lock him in a room?" When he spied a dog on the street, he hid behind his companion or ran away. However, he continued to go out, played outdoors, and visited his friends. His fear of dogs did not interfere with his activities. After several months the fear began to diminish and finally disappeared.

Four-year-old Susan developed a similar fear after she was knocked down by a dog. When this happened she already had a number of other fears—fear of her mother leaving her, fear of the dark, fear of strangers. After the frightening experience with the dog, she refused to go visiting anyone with or without her mother lest there be a dog. The fear of dogs became one of a number of fears which restricted her activities and experiences more and more as she grew older.

These pointers are not intended as a definitive guide to home diagnosis of behavior problems, which would indeed be impossible. Rather, they are offered to help parents mark out some of the boundaries between normal and abnormal behavior in children. The most common mistake parents make is not failure to see trouble, but delay in doing something about it.

Sometimes a father or mother will worry over a child who isn't getting along the way they think he should, almost decide to do something, change their minds because he *seems* to be getting better, only to find a few weeks later that nothing really has changed. They continue this vacillation, never really happy about the child's progress, never really sure they should get advice.

It is better to consider consultation with a qualified professional as a first-aid measure rather than as a court of last resort. If a child were to complain of pains in his side off and on for a week or two, there isn't a parent who wouldn't take him for a medical check-up. The same should be true when the difficulties are emotional and behavioral. Whatever the diagnosis is, everyone will benefit from an objective opinion. At best, the parent will find his worries groundless. At worst, he will have taken the first step toward helping the child out of the difficulties that are blocking his healthy growth as a person.

Some parents are afraid to consult a psychiatrist because they have heard that no matter what the child's problem may be the psychiatrist will always recommend long and expensive treatment. This is not the case. The great majority of children's problems can be and are handled effectively by simple parent guidance. A change in parent handling to make it more suitable for the child's temperament or relieving excess pressure either at home or in school may be sufficient to accomplish dramatic improvement. In our research study many of the parents have consulted us when problem behavior has developed in the children. In over 80 per cent of such consultations, guidance and advice have been sufficient. Only in a small minority has long treatment of the child been necessary.

When should one call the doctor? Whenever the parents are worried for any length of time. Another good rule-of-thumb is to get advice whenever parent-child relations are such that tension is the dominant theme and relaxed enjoyment of the child is becoming increasingly infrequent. Such a developing negative atmosphere is a signal that something is wrong. The problem may be serious, in which case treatment is certainly indicated. If it is minor, guidance and advice may help to eliminate it quickly and easily.

23 THE MANY
WAYS OF PARENTHOOD

Parents—as a harried mother once pleaded—are people, too. They share the human characteristic of being different. They are at least as different from one another as are their children.

Men and women vary enormously in the way they play their parental roles. This is not surprising. Adults are first of all different individuals before they become parents. Then they have children who differ in all kinds of ways: temperament, intellectual level, rate of development, state of health. Finally, the demands of being a parent create many changes in their previous way of life, changes that will vary in kind and degree from one parent to another. The reaction of the parent to his specific child and to his altered way of life adds a new dimension to his character. New personality characteristics may appear, some old ones may be intensified, and others diminished.

One mother may never have seen a relative take care of children and run a house. Another may never have seen a woman in her family do anything else. One father may have come from a family that didn't believe girls need higher education. Another may have come from a family where boys and girls were taught to aspire to intellectual careers, and were ignored or praised, alike, regardless of sex.

Some parents were poor children; some were rich. Some went to dancing school; some thought dancing school was for sissies. Some came from families where father knew best; some from families where mother was the chief executive. In some families all recreation was family recreation; other families were more formal, with children's times and grownups' times.

Education will affect what a mother does with her spare time, her approach to motherhood, and her reaction to the demands of her children at various stages of their development. The value parents put on children's school performance will be influenced by their own interest and involvement in education.

When people become parents they already have well-defined interests that affect the way they live their lives. Painting, bowling, chess, music, baseball, watching television, and other interests, whether weak or strong, many or few, will influence them as parents, just as they distinguish them as people.

The nature of their jobs, their work schedule, and the way they talk about their work at home are important. A father's relationship with his children will differ from the usual if he has a night job or has to travel a lot. If he is absorbed in his job and talks about it enthusiastically at home, his children may be influenced differently from children whose father's work is dull and monotonous so that he is always grumbling about it.

Group cultural attitudes and standards influence parental standards and expectations. Sometimes, if they aspire to a higher social class, this will cause them to make special demands on their children.

A most distinctive characteristic of each parent's way of parenthood stems from his individual personality. The adult is not just a grown-up version of his baby self, but a complex personality formed out of continuous interaction with the environment in which he grew up.

The range of normal personality traits is vast. Many people have harmful traits which result from neurosis or other psychiatric problems. They may be exaggerations of normal trends such as resistance to change to the point of being compulsively rigid, or shyness that leads almost to social isolation. Or they may be special traits, such as guilt-reactions, excessive dependency on others, marked fearfulness, suspiciousness of people, etc. An unhealthy personality characteristic sometimes intrudes very little on the parental role. In other instances it interferes seriously and damages the whole course of the child's development.

Parenthood often changes a mother's way of life drastically. She may have previously been a worker in the outside world, meeting new people and doing new things each day. At home with her baby she is cut off from most adult society and finds that her work is much more repetitious and physically demanding. Her social activities, as well as her husband's, may be curtailed. On the positive side she now has the responsibility for her child's well-being and the satisfaction of watching his growth and development.

Parenthood may change the father's life too. Evenings, weekends, and vacations may no longer be the same as before. Pressures for earning a better living may jump tremendously. Positive involvement with his children may add a new special dimension of enjoyment to life.

All these influences will affect what a parent considers important: how much time he spends with his children, what he does with them, what he makes issues over, what he lets slide, how he reacts to each child at each moment of their joint experience.

The child's temperamental characteristics may strongly influence parental feelings and behavior. Tired or chronically ill parents may find it much easier to accept and love fully an easily adaptable and quiet child than a loud, very active and irregular one whose care is much more demanding. Lively, energetic parents may be more quickly responsive to a child like themselves than to a slow-moving quiet youngster.

There are some universal requirements for good parenthood.

Good parents plan room in their lives for a child. A father who works so hard to give his son material advantages that he has no time left to give to the boy is not being a father to him. A mother who tries to manage her social life (out every evening) and her household (no room where a child can act like a child) as if a baby were just a portable object can't begin to be an adequate mother.

Good parents clearly, simply, and directly communicate their feelings, attitudes, standards, and demands. What they communicate to the child is personally and socially healthy, appropriate to the situation, to the child's level of development, and to his temperament. This means showing disapproval plainly when children behave badly or disobey; showing anger when disobedience and bad behavior are clearly intentional; reacting with approval at efforts to please, to learn, to correct mistakes; showing appreciation for consideration and affection; and being broadly consistent in demands and responses. It doesn't mean *never* overlooking a misstep or *never* getting angry without reason. It doesn't mean *always* being attentive to a child's efforts to show his love and longing to please. Parents can make lots of mistakes. They can scream with fury over almost nothing at all, threaten and deliver punishments that are inappropriate, if not undeserved. But as long as the general tenor of their relations with their children is reasonably kind and sensible, and they are aware of their mistakes and able to correct them, they won't inflict irreparable damage.

Within these universals there is room for the widest expression of individuality. Parents benefit when they can be themselves, and so do their children. But parents cannot feel free to express their own individualities if they are striving toward mythical and unattainable standards. A mother who feels she must be a kind of Caesar's wife, above reproach, or otherwise her child will suffer, is the victim of clichés about parenthood.

The most popular cliché is that the parent must give love at all times and in all ways. If a parent puts his own interests, needs, or wishes first at any time, the child is in danger of feeling unloved or rejected. According to this formula, the working mother, the mother who goes out in spite of her child's protests, the father who prefers Bach to children's records, are all equally culpable.

By this standard, the mother who shows disapproval when a child drops his brother's teddy bear out the window or bullies his friends may be rejecting him. Expecting high standards for schoolwork is to be considered dangerous. It may make a child feel that he is loved only for performance and not for himself, so the formula would go.

To say that children need love is to belabor the obvious. An unloved and unwanted child is a tragic and innocent victim of his parents and society. But the bland prescription of love and more love as an emotional panacea for all parent-child issues is quite another matter.

Is it really desirable for a parent to tell a child that nothing he does will affect his parent's feelings? Is it wise to encourage a youngster to think that what he does and says to other people will not change their feelings toward him?

The pat formula of unlimited love and acceptance ignores the child's need to face life and adapt to the fact that, while he may be unique, he is only one of many human beings in the world. Parents who try to follow this formula may find themselves acting a part instead of being themselves. They will not be able to give their children the best they have to offer: their own individual flavor, the benefit of their particular life experiences, and the meaningfulness of their own approach to living.

A zoologist spends days in the woods with his four-year-old son, Sam, looking under stones, watching for birds, catching tadpoles to bring home and raise. The dedicated parents next door cluck in disapproval as they take their four-year-old Bobby to his weekly finger-painting session, an activity they consider far more appropriate to his "developmental level."

They feel sorry for Sam, hanging around his father all day, alone in the woods. Sam's father, at the same time, feels sorry for Bobby's parents, always sacrificing their own interests in favor of what is "good" for their children.

Which parents are right? No pat answer is possible. If Sam likes being in the woods, he will get a great deal out of beginning to share his father's interests. If Sam, however, really dislikes being out all day without companions of his own age, he may resent the lonely expeditions to the woods. If Bobby enjoys finger painting and it helps develop a spontaneity of expression he had lacked, his parents' devotion will be worth-while. If he doesn't want to finger-paint and goes reluctantly, his parents would do better not to sacrifice their time for it.

Parents can be different or react differently to different children and still be loving.

A mother who enjoyed playing with her son more than with her daughter came to us because she thought her preference would turn the boy into a homosexual and make her daughter feel rejected. The boy was a light-hearted, responsive, very active youngster. His sister was temperamentally quiet and solemn. The mother was affectionate and attentive to both children. She responded more actively to the boy simply because he engaged her attention more easily. Actually, the little girl responded in the same positive way to her brother's infectious gaiety. When the mother realized that the boy's outgoing temperament provided a healthy stimulus for her and for his sister, she began to enjoy her children as she had originally, before stereotypes about what is proper in parent-child relationships had made her feel guilty.

Another cliché is that if a parent has unloving feelings, anxieties, or conflicts about parenthood, the child will sense these and suffer. This is only true if the parent communicates his feelings by his behavior. Grownups do not have to act out unloving thoughts, even when they have them. The normal adult will not punish children for suffering, frustration, or disappointment they have no part in. A mother may confess disappointment or frustration: "I wish I could have taken that job, but I wouldn't want to be away from the baby that much." But she doesn't slap the baby or deprive him of attention and affection because he interfered with her career. A father may feel badly that his son is not athletic, but that doesn't mean he goads him for being clumsy or makes fun of him for being a bookworm or tries to make him go out for sports.

The impulse to protect and nurture one's children is so strong, in fact, that we have even seen mothers and fathers who are severely handicapped by neurotic problems try to control themselves for their children's sakes.

One mother who was so anxious that she literally could not let her four-year-old son out of her sight came to us for help. She wanted to learn to control her fears so that she would not transmit them to her child. She was so anxious a person that she was too terrified to try the kind of psychotherapy needed in order to try to master her neurosis. But her concern for the child made it possible for her to follow the very gradual steps we outlined for letting go of him.

First, she left him alone at nursery school. Next, she let him go alone on the school bus. Then, she let him go down on the elevator, get the bus by himself, and come back to the apartment alone after school. Finally, she let him visit other children overnight.

With each new step the boy took, the mother's anxiety increased temporarily. But she was able to steel herself, smile, wave good-bye to him, and then wait tensely until he returned home. Helped by his mother's behavior, the son developed confidence and assurance while she continued to be as fearful and insecure as ever.

Unfortunately, not all parents with psychiatric problems can control their behavior as effectively as this mother did. Many require professional help before they can learn to avoid damaging their children by their actions.

Just as there are many kinds of *good* parents, there are many kinds of *bad* parents. A mother may use a child as a status symbol or as a pawn in a hostile battle with her husband. A father may try to live vicariously through his son and pressure the boy to live out successfully his own frustrated ambitions. In general, whenever a parent subordinates the legitimate needs of the child to some unhealthy goal or destructive activity of his own, the child is likely to suffer. The damage done may vary greatly, depending on the combination of the parent's behavior and the child's temperamental reaction characteristics. But unless the parents take steps to change their behavior the outcome for the child is always a matter of deep concern.

There is no mystery about good parenthood. If parents cultivate with their children the qualities they use to make their other close and deep relationships work, there will probably be no need to worry about whether the child is sufficiently loved.

Sometimes parents seem so weighed down with instructions and commandments that the joys of parenthood are quite obscured. This is indeed sad. Children are one of the most reliable and richest sources of pleasure in life.

It is fun for parents to observe how long the baby, at five weeks, holds up his head, to see his reaction when he first tastes a new food, to catch the way he looks when he sees himself in the mirror for the first time, or to watch a determined two-year-old trying to cut meat or tie his shoes.

It is fun to teach children to do the things you enjoy and introduce them to books and ideas and interests that mean a lot to you, and to see flashes of a father's wit or a mother's charm appearing in the child.

Parents who enjoy their children in their own individual ways can be sure the children are also benefiting. If there is one thing above all that children will thrive on, it is their parents' pleasure in them.

REFERENCE NOTES

I: THE PARENTS' DILEMMA

1. G. Gurin, J. Veroff, and S. Feld, *Americans View Their Mental Health* (New York: Basic Books, 1960), pp. 141–142.
2. H. Bruch, "Parent Education, or the Illusion of Omnipotence," *American Journal of Orthopsychiatry*, 24:723 (1954).
3. S. Escalona, in *Problems of Infancy and Childhood* (New York: Josiah Macy, Jr., Foundation, 1952), p. 46.
4. A. M. Johnson and S. A. Szurek, "The Genesis of Anti-Social Acting-Out in Children and Adults," *Psychoanalytic Quarterly*, 21:323 (1952).
5. M. Kris, "The Use of Prediction in a Longitudinal Study," *Psychoanalytic Study of the Child*, 12:175 (1957).
6. M. Mahler, "Thoughts About Development and Individuation," *Psychoanalytic Study of the Child*, 18:307 (1963).
7. E. Pavenstedt, "A Study of Immature Mothers and Their Children," in *Prevention of Mental Disorders in Children*, G. Caplan, editor (New York: Basic Books, 1961), p. 195.
8. J. L. Hymes, Jr., "Relearning What 'Permissive' Means," *New York Times Sunday Magazine* (Oct. 27, 1963), p. 91.
9. L. Robbins, "The Accuracy of Parental Recall of Aspects of Child Development and of Child-Rearing Practices," *Journal of Abnormal and Social Psychology*, 66:261 (1963).
10. C. Wenar, "The Reliability of Developmental Histories," *Psychosomatic Medicine*, 25:505 (1963).
11. S. Chess, A. Thomas, and H. G. Birch, "Distortions in Developmental Reporting Made by Parents of Behaviorally Disturbed Children," *Journal Academy of Child Psychiatry*, in press.
12. J. D. Frank, *Persuasion and Healing* (Baltimore: The Johns Hopkins Press, 1961).
13. H. R. Beiser, "Discrepancies in the Symptomatology of Parents and Children," *Journal of the American Academy of Child Psychiatry*, 3:457 (1964).

14. H. Orlansky, "Infant Care and Personality," *Psychological Bulletin*, 46:1 (1949).
15. E. H. Klatskin, E. B. Jackson, and L. C. Wilkin, "The Influence of Degree of Flexibility in Maternal Child Care Practices on Early Child Behavior," *American Journal of Orthopsychiatry*, 26:79 (1956).
16. H. R. Schaffer and P. E. Emerson, "The Development of Social Attachments in Infancy," *Monographs of the Society for Research in Child Development*, 29:3, 72 (1964).

II: THE SEARCH FOR ALTERNATIVES

1. J. B. Watson, *Behaviorism* (New York: W. W. Norton, 1924).
2. A. Gesell and L. B. Ames, "Early Evidences of Individuality in the Hu man Infant," *Journal of Genetic Psychology*, 47:339 (1937).
3. M. M. Shirley, *The First Two Years: A Study of Twenty-Five Babies* (Minneapolis: University of Minnesota Press, 1931 and 1933).
4. H. L. Witmer and R. Kotinsky (editors), "Personality in the Making," in *Fact-Finding Report of Mid-Century White House Conference on Children and Youth* (New York: Harper and Brothers, 1952), p. 35.
5. See A. Thomas, S. Chess, H. G. Birch, and others, *Behavioral Individuality in Early Childhood* (New York: New York University Press, 1963), Introduction, for references to these studies.
6. L. B. Murphy and Associates, *The Widening World of Childhood* (New York: Basic Books, 1962).

VI: BREAST OR BOTTLE?

1. A. Montague, "Culture and Mental Illness," *American Journal of Psychiatry*, 118:17 (1961).
2. M. I. Heinstein, "Behavioral Correlates of Breast-Bottle Regimes under Varying Parent-Infant Relationships," *Monographs of the Society for Research in Child Development*, 28:4, 53 (1963).
3. R. R. Sears and G. W. Wise, "Relation of Cup Feeding to Thumbsucking and the Oral Drive," *American Journal of Orthopsychiatry*, 20:123 (1950).
4. R. E. Davis and R. E. Ruiz, "Infant Feeding Method and Adolescent Personality," presented at Annual Meeting of the American Psychiatric Association, New York City (May 5, 1965).

IX: THE END OF DIAPERS

1. J. L. Hymes, *The Child Under Six* (New York: Prentice-Hall, 1963), p. 111.
2. J. Dollard and N. E. Miller, *Personality and Psychotherapy* (New York: McGraw-Hill, 1950), pp. 137–139.
3. E. H. Erikson, *Childhood and Society* (New York: W. W. Norton, 1950), p. 77.

XVI: A NEW BABY ARRIVES

1. E. H. Erikson, op. cit., p. 75.

XIX: THE WORKING MOTHER: NOT GUILTY!

1. A. Kardiner, *Sex and Morality* (Indianapolis: Bobbs-Merrill Company, 1954), pp. 223–225.
2. J. Bowlby, *Child Care and the Growth of Love* (Middlesex: Penguin Books, 1953).
3. *Deprivation of Maternal Care, A Reassessment of Its Effects,* Public Health Papers 14, World Health Organization, Geneva, 1962.
4. N. O'Connor and C. M. Franks, "Childhood Upbringing and Other Environmental Factors," in *Handbook of Abnormal Psychology,* H. J. Eysenck, editor (New York: Basic Books, 1961), p. 400.
5. H. S. Maas, "The Young Adult Adjustment of Twenty Wartime Residential Nursery Children," *Child Welfare,* Feb. 1963.
6. L. J. Yarrow, "Maternal Deprivation: Toward an Empirical and Conceptual Reevaluation," *Psychological Bulletin,* 58:477 (1961).
7. A. E. Siegel and M. B. Hass, "The Working Mother: A Review of Research," *Child Development,* 34:538 (1963).
8. L. M. Stolz, "Effects of Maternal Employment on Children: Evidence from Research," *Child Development,* 31:779 (1960).
9. A. E. Siegel and M. B. Hass, op. cit.

XXI: THE HANDICAPPED CHILD

1. A recent book by Dr. Benjamin Spock and Dr. M. Lerrigo, *Caring for Your Disabled Child* (New York: The Macmillan Co., 1965) offers a complete guide for the care of the handicapped child and a detailed, listing of the many agencies available to help parents.
2. See H. G. Birch and L. Belmont, "The Problem of Comparing Home Rearing Versus Foster-Home Rearing in Defective Children," *Pediatrics,* 28:956 (1961), for an analysis of the issue of home care versus institutional care in defective children.

INDEX

Abnormality: physical, 177–78, 179–86; psychological, 59, 110, 133, 135–37, 152, 169–70, 173, 187–95

Active child, 41–43, 86; and manners, 103; and new situations, 114; and play, 136–47; and school, 156–65; and toilet training, 83; *see also* Activity

Activity, 33; high, 28, 41–43; moderate, 39; low, 28; *see also* Active child

Adaptability, 19, 29, 41, 51; *see also* Adaptable child; Difficult child; Easy child; Nonadaptable child; "Slow Warmer-Up"

Adaptable child, 100, 174, 177; and feeding, 69, 70; and learning, 157–58, 165; and new baby, 140, 144; and new situations, 112–21; and nursery school, 150–51; and obedience (rules), 92–95; retarded, 182–83; and talking, 175; *see also* Easy child

Adjustment, 188–89; *see also* Adaptable child; Nonadaptable child

American Journal of Psychiatry, 62

Anal phase of personality development, 6, 7, 17

Anxiety, 4, 5, 114, 167, 174, 201

Appetite, 73

Attention span, *see* Persistence

Authority, 87

Behavior problems, 176, 187–95

Behaviorism, 18–20

Beiser, Helen, 13

Belmont, L. (cited), 182

Birch, H. G. (cited), 182

Bottle feeding, *see* Feeding; Weaning

Bowel elimination, 55, 83; *see also* Toilet training

Bowlby, J. (cited), 169

Breast feeding, *see* Feeding

Bruch, Hilde, 5, 6

Change, *see* New Situations

Charm, 40

Clarity (in training), 90, 97, 104

Clinging, 191–92

Competition, 18

Consistency, 49, 52, 199; and difficult child, 125; and discipline, 90–91; and feeding, 74, 79; and manners, 103; and rules, 94; and sleeping, 52, 55–56, 60

Constipation, 85

Constitutionalism, 16–17

Co-ordination, muscular, 176–77

Criticism (and discipline), 91

Crying, 3, 59–60, 86; and discipline, 88; and fear, 121; and hunger, 56,

Crying (*continued*)
   69–71; of irregular child, 56; *see also* Tantrums
Cultural school of psychoanalysis, 18, 20
Cup feeding, *see* Feeding
Curiosity, 107–108, 111, 158

Davis, R. E. (cited), 64
Defective child, *see* Handicapped child
Dependency, 197
Deutsch, Helene, 168
Diarrhea, 85–86
Difficult child, 37–39, 78–80, 122–130, 159; *see also* "Slow Warmer-Up"
Diffident child, *see* "Slow Warmer-Up"
Discipline, 87–104; *see also* Obedience; Rules
Distractible child, 31, 48, 103, 154, 156–65
Disturbance, psychological, *see* Abnormality, psychological
Dollard, J. (quoted), 81
Dreams, 58; *see also* Nightmares
Drop-outs, 157

Easy child, 39–41, 48–49, 53–54, 123, 157–58; *see also* Adaptable child
Eating, *see* Feeding
Education, 146–65; sexual, 106, 111
Emerson, P. E. (quoted), 14
Emotional problems, 59, 187–95
Encouragement (positive reinforcement), 91, 94, 95
Environment, 16–21, 23, 24, 27, 185; and discipline, 89; and manners, 102, 104; and weaning, 77, 78
Erikson, E. H. (quoted), 81, 138
Escalona, S. (quoted), 8
Expressive child, 96; *see also* Intense child

Fear, 190, 193; and new situations, 120; and play, 121, 132, 135; and weaning, 78
Feeding, 61–80; and anal phase, 76; anxiety and, 74; bottle, 51, 61–67, 75; breast, 61–63, 64–65; cup, 63, 64, 75–80; on demand, 3; and distractions, 73–74; fads in, 74; formula, 61–66; and irregular child, 55, 56, 69; and problem child, 78–79, 125; psychoanalytic theory on, 63–64, 76; and oral phase, 76; ready-to-serve foods, 68; and rules, 103; and self-demand, 69–70; self-feeding, 140, 161; and spoon, 72, 73; sucking activity, 64; and thumb-sucking, 76; and toilet training, 6; *see also* Weaning
Feld, S. (cited), 5
Femininity, 168, 171
Flexibility, 49
Food, *see* Feeding
Formula feeding, *see* Feeding
Frank, Jerome D., 13
Franks, C. M. (cited), 169
Freud, Sigmund, 6, 17, 18, 19, 21, 76, 105, 106, 168
Fromm, Erich, 18, 107
Frustration: and behavior problems, 176; and learning, 89–90; of parents, 167; and restraint, 7, 175; and toilet training, 81–82

Genital phase of personality development, 6, 7, 17
Gesell, Arnold, 19, 20, 22
Gregarious child, 133, 144, 156
Growth: physical, 73; psychological, 82
Guilt (shame), 180–82, 197
Gurin, G. (cited), 5

Habits, 77; *see also* Routines
Handicapped child, 179–86
Hass. M. B. (quoted), 170

Heinstein, Martin I., 63
Heterosexual development, 7
Homework, 165
Horney, Karen, 107
Hymes, J. L., 10 (quoted), 81

Illness, 53, 56, 58, 59, 73
Independence, 186
Influences in child development, 16–22
Insatiable child, 144
Institute for Juvenile Research (Chicago), 13
Institutions (for handicapped child), 185–86
Intelligence, 157, 165
Intense child, 33, 57, 70, 140
Interaction (between constitutional factors and environment), 20, 25
Irregular child, 60, 84–85, 123; and feeding, 54–57, 69; and sleeping, 54–57; and toilet training, 83, 84–85

Jackson, Edith, 14
Joint Commission on Mental Health and Illness, 5
Johnson, A. M. (quoted), 8
Juvenile delinquency, 8

Kardiner, A. (quoted), 166
Klatskin, E. H. (quoted), 14
Kotinsky, R., ed. (cited), 22
Kris, M. (quoted), 9

Language, *see* Talking
"Late blooming" child, 173–77
Learning, 202; and discipline, 89–90; and manners, 100; *see also* Education; Nursery school
Lerrigo, M. (cited), 180
Lessons, 103; *see also* Learning
Libido, 6–7
Locke, John, 16

Mass, H. S. (cited), 170
Mahler, Margaret, 10
Manners, 90, 99–104, 110; *see also* Rules
Masterful child, 134
Masturbation, 106, 109–10
McIntosh, Millicent, 6
Mental illness, 187–95; *see also* Abnormality, psychological
Mid-Century White House Conference on Children and Youth (1950), 22
Mild (quiet) child, 123, 177; and discipline, 96; and feeding, 57, 70–71; handicapped, 182–83; and new baby, 140; and new situations, 114; and play, 133–34; and sleeping, 57; and talking, 175; and toilet training, 83
Miller, N. E. (quoted), 81
Minding, *see* Obedience
Modesty, 105–11
Montague, A. (quoted), 62
Mood: negative, 30–31, 37–38, 123; positive, 30–31, 38
Murphy, Lois, 22

Nakedness, 105, 106, 109
Negative child, 191; and learning, 156–57, 159; and new situations, 116; and sex, 110; and sleeping, 58; and talking, 175; *see also* Difficult child
New situations (change), 93, 112–121, 123, 192; child's approach to, 28; and feeding, 72, 74, 78; at school, 162; and sleeping, 51–53, 57–58; withdrawal from, 28; *see also* Weaning; Toilet training
New York Longitudinal Study of Child Development, 23; classifications in, 28–32; methods used in, 25–27, 33–34; questions raised in, 24–25; subjects of, 25; temperament and, 32–34

Nightmares, 58, 193
Noise, 58
Nonadaptable child, 55, 57; and feeding, 69; and new baby, 140, 144; and new situations, 112–121; and nursery school, 150; retarded, 183; *see also* Difficult child
Nondistractible child, 44–46, 47; *see also* Persistent child
Nonpersistent child, 159–60
Nursery school, 117–18, 131, 146–155, 156–65, 192
Nursing, *see* Feeding

Obedience (minding), 87–98, 129, 198
Obesity, 181
O'Connor, N. (cited), 169
One-track child, 151
Oral phase of personality development, 6, 7, 17
Orlansky, Harold, 13
Overambitious child, 136
Overattentiveness, 53–54
Overprotection, 175, 180

Pavenstedt, E. (quoted), 10
Pavlov, Ivan, 17, 20, 21
Persistence, 32
Persistent child, 44–48, 174, 177; and learning, 156–65; and play, 134; and rules, 93–94; and sleeping, 57
"Person-oriented" child, 164
Personality: constitutionalist view of, 16–17; environmentalist view of, 16, 17; heterosexual development of, 7; psychoanalytic theory and, 6–7, 12–15, 17, 18, 19; social development of, 7; variations in, 20–23
Persuasion and Healing (Frank), 13
Piaget, Jean, 19, 20
Piecemeal learners, 164, 165
Play, 33, 131–37; abnormal, 135–37, 191; in new situations, 113, 117–118, 120–21; *see also* Nursery school
Politeness, *see* Manners
Positive child, 93, 175, 182–83; and new baby, 140; in new situations, 113, 114; retarded, 182–83; at school, 150, 157; and weaning, 78; *see also* Active child
Pressure, 46, 116
Problem child, *see* Difficult child
Protest, *see* Crying; Tantrums
Prudery, 106
Psychiatrists, 194–95
Psychology of Women, The (Helene Deutsch), 168
Psychosis, *see* Abnormality, psychological
Punishment, 85, 90, 96–97, 125, 127

Quiet child, *see* Mild child

Reading, 47, 147, 165, 175, 176
Reflexes, conditioned, 17, 20
Regular child: and feeding, 69; and sleeping, 50; and toilet training, 83–84
Regularity, 28
"Reliability of Developmental Histories, The," 12
Response, 31; *see also* Intensity
Restraint, 7; *see also* Frustration
Rigidity (and discipline), 90
Routines (schedules), 53, 56, 60, 126, 128–29; and feeding, 68–71; and new baby, 140–41; and sleeping, 10–12, 51, 56–59; *see also* Rules
Ruiz, R. E. (cited), 64
Rules, 57, 87–98, 165; *see also* Routines

Safety, 88; in street crossing, 92, 94
Schaffer, H. R. (quoted), 14
Schedules, *see* Routines
Sears, R. R. (cited), 63

Selective child, 153
Self-demand (in feeding), 69–70
Sensory threshold, 30
Sex, 105–11
Sexual development, 6–7
Shirley, Mary, 22
Shyness (timidity), 103, 114, 188, 191
Sibling rivalry, 138–45
Siegel, A. E. (quoted), 170
Sleeping, 50–60; and feeding, 56; patterns, 11; problems, 51–52, 55–56, 190, 192; and waking (cycle), 57
Sleeplessness, 3–5, 10–12, 86, 190
"Slow Warmer-Up," 35–37; and learning, 164; and new situations, 115–119; and nursery school, 150–51, 153; and play, 134–35
Social customs, *see* Manners
Social experience, 92, 142, 175, 188–189; *see also* Nursery school; Play
Solitary child, 133, 152–53, 154
Spock, Benjamin (cited), 180
Spoon, use of, 72, 73
Stereotypes (clichés), 131, 149, 152, 155, 172, 188–90, 100, 201
Stolz, L. M. (quoted), 170
Story-telling (at bedtime), 52
Sucking activity, 64
Sullivan, Harry Stack, 107
Suspiciousness, 197
Szurek, S. A. (quoted), 8

Talking (language), 84, 173–78, 183
Tantrums, 37–39, 46, 47, 129; and

emotional disturbance, 188, 191; of "late bloomer," 176; and mistakes, 137; in new situations, 112, 115, 118–19; and obedience, 93; and sleeping, 52
"Task-oriented" child, 163–64
Tears, *see* Crying
Teething, 53, 58
Temperament (described), 32–33, 34
Thompson, Clara, 107
Thumb-sucking, 76, 106, 127, 192
Timidity, *see* Shyness
Toilet training, 7, 9, 47, 81–86, 139, 183
Tying shoelaces, 91

Unconscious, the (of parents), 6–10
University of California, 63
University of Iowa, 63

Veroff, J. (cited), 5

Walking, 91, 173–78, 184, 190
Watson, John B., 17, 18, 20
Weaning, 7, 47, 75–80
Weeping, *see* Crying
Wenar, C. (quoted), 12
Widening World of Childhood, The (Murphy), 22
Wilkin, L. C. (quoted), 14
Wise, G. W. (cited), 63
Witmer, H. L., ed. (cited), 22
Working mother, 166–72
Writing, 175

Yarrow, L. J. (cited), 170